Brain Men

Also by Marcus Berkmann

Rain Men: The Madness of Cricket

Brain Men

A Passion to Compete

MARCUS BERKMANN

LITTLE, BROWN AND COMPANY

A *Little, Brown* Book

First published in Great Britain by
Little, Brown and Company 1999

Copyright © Marcus Berkmann 1999

The moral right of the author has been asserted.

A CIP catalogue record for this book
is available from the British Library.

ISBN 0 316 84769 0

Typeset in Janson by M Rules
Printed and bound in Great Britain by
Clays Ltd, St Ives plc

Little, Brown and Company (UK)
Brettenham House
Lancaster Place
London WC2E 7EN

To Paula

Contents

'For knowledge itself is power.'

(FRANCIS BACON)

'If it rained knowledge, I'd hold out my hand; but I would not give myself the trouble to go in quest of it.'

(SAMUEL JOHNSON)

'It is a good thing for an uneducated man to read books of quotations.'

(SIR WINSTON CHURCHILL)

1
'Nick'

'What is the answer? . . . In that case, what is the question?'

(Gertrude Stein's last words)

Several years ago I went along to the launch of a book of essays about football, a copy of which you may well own, since it later sold in the sort of quantities that make rival publishers weep with anger. Many of the country's best and brightest young writers were at the launch, as well as a newspaper executive who had recently fired me, several TV commentators who were saying 'fuck' a lot and the usual sprinkling of frauds, bores and hangers-on. After wandering around for a while wishing I was dead, I persuaded the contributor who had invited me to introduce me to the book's editor, a slight, balding figure who had recently enjoyed a notable success with another book about football, and has since become one of the richest and most widely admired novelists on the planet. We shall call him 'Nick'.

'Ah, "Nick",' said my friend to the young doyen. 'Can I introduce you to Marcus Berkmann, who's an old friend of mine.'

'Nick' turned round and looked at me. I burbled some heartfelt appreciation of his previous bestseller, although I don't think he heard a word. 'Nick' was staring at me in much the same way that headmasters stare at you after you have narrowly failed to burn down the science block. My burbling subsided. There was an awkward silence.

'I know you,' said 'Nick' suddenly. 'You were in the team that beat us every week in the quiz at the Cock Tavern.'

'Was I?' I began, delighted by this information, but 'Nick' had already turned away to talk to someone else. Had I said another word I would have been addressing the back of his head. The conversation was at an end. I had been dismissed. I had been a member of the team that had regularly beaten his team in the quiz at the Cock Tavern on Great Portland Street, London W1, in late 1991 and early 1992. Three years later he was still furious about it. Fame and glory had embraced him since, but those Cock Tavern wounds had not healed. I was astonished. After all, we hadn't won the quiz every week. Sometimes we had come second.

I should stress that this 'Nick' is renowned in media circles and beyond for his kindness, generosity and good nature. I don't think I have ever heard anyone speak ill of him, which, given his vast wealth, is not a bad record. And yet pub quizzes seemed to be his Achilles heel. (Had Achilles ever taken part in a pub quiz, he might have been equally put out, especially when questions came up about his heel, of which he obviously knew nothing. Similar problems have been faced by the cast of *EastEnders* whenever the Queen Vic has held its own quiz. For only in Albert Square's premier boozer could there be a pub quiz without any questions about *EastEnders*. Asking which actor played Arthur Fowler, for example, would be met only by blank looks, and several dropped points all round.)

Does it matter that we usually beat 'Nick' and his team? Of course it does. If it didn't, none of us would have bothered to turn up every week, and I wouldn't have remembered that it was in late 1991 and early 1992 without having to look it up.

Just because pub quizzes aren't important doesn't mean they don't matter. As it is, I believe 'Nick' had his finger on the nation's pulse as always. Indeed, it's probably just as well for me that he didn't think of writing this book before I did.

For the pub quiz is a far broader social phenomenon than it is often given credit for. In its quiet, undemonstrative way – and in a remarkably short time – it has become a cornerstone of British cultural life. Football makes all the money. Literature, cinema and the plastic arts hog the column inches. Television fuels the most pub conversations. But what are these people doing in the pub, as they discuss the latest episode of *Blind Date*? Waiting for the quiz to start, of course. Thousands upon thousands of people take part in pub quizzes every week, answering questions on football, literature, cinema and television, as well as Henry VIII's six wives. (The first? The last? The longest lived? The shortest marriage? The first to bear him a child? The one whose heart was hidden in a church in Thetford, Suffolk, for 300 years? The only one who, when she married him, was both a widow and a virgin?[1])

To the heaving mass of non-quizzers, this may seem quite a daft way of passing the time. Who cares who won the League Cup in 1972?[2] Such knowledge doesn't feed the soul,

---

[1] The first: Catherine of Aragon. The last: Catherine Parr. The longest lived: Catherine of Aragon (51). The shortest marriage: Anne of Cleves (six months). The first to bear a child: Catherine of Aragon (her daughter later became Mary I). The one whose heart was hidden in a church: Anne Boleyn. The widow and virgin: Catherine of Aragon again, who had been married before to Henry's older brother Arthur. Consummating the union may not have been such a high priority in those days.

[2] Stoke City supporters probably care the most, as their team beat Chelsea 2–1.

and it certainly won't feed the family. But you might as well ask why people love crown green bowls or Curly Wurlys or anything that has no practical value. For most of us the pub quiz is a weekly social ritual that just happens to involve answering several dozen quiz questions. We don't really know why we do it, and we don't much care. But we do know that the chemical symbol for tungsten is W.

Let's be frank here. Within its narrow bounds, a pub quiz is a serious business. Fifteen, maybe twenty pounds may be at stake. Your knowledge of international car registration letters could be tested to its very limit. Answers that you were sure were right will turn out to be wrong. Answers you knew to be wrong but did not dare say so will turn out to be wrong. Drink will dull your senses and ruin your digestion. By the end of the evening you will be gritting your teeth with the frustration of it all, and rushing to the toilet every seven-and-a-half minutes. Then a week later you and your friends will come back and do the same thing all over again.

This pattern is repeated in pubs and clubs across Britain, in quiz leagues and cups and plates and shields, in grand celebrity quizzes for charity, in money-raising quizzes in church and village halls; and by extension, in abstruse quizzes by mail, in a stream of quiz shows on radio and TV, in newspapers and magazines and kids' comics, and in inconsequential conversations between friends. What breed of dog was Scooby Doo? For every five people who immediately know the answer,[3] there will be five more who will say it's on the tip of their tongue ('No, don't tell me, I'll get it in a minute'). Only a few crabbed individuals, narrow of mind and stony of heart, will turn their noses up and ask why anyone would possibly be interested in such a thing. But then not everyone watched

---

[3] A Great Dane.

Scooby Doo as a child. Perhaps *Magpie* was on the other side at the same time.

Britain's quiz culture is thriving. And it is a British thing, this passion to compete. I have heard of pub quizzes (or their local equivalents) in Australia and New Zealand, in South Africa and many old British colonies in Africa, in Hong Kong and Gibraltar and anywhere else where English is spoken in a broadly unAmerican way. But I have found no equivalent in the US, for instance, and absolutely nothing in continental Europe that isn't run by British expatriates. Foreigners clearly have more (or less) important things to do. Or maybe it has never occurred to them that this might be an amusing way of frittering away their valuable leisure time. I once took some American tourists to a pub quiz. They couldn't believe their eyes. They had expected Britain and the British to be eccentric, but never for a moment had they ever imagined that grown men and women would voluntarily sit in pubs once a week and write down answers to general knowledge questions on photocopied sheets. 'And I thought Stonehenge was weird,' said one man.

We don't export it, and we keep it fairly quiet over here as well. For such a popular activity the pub quiz keeps an unusually low profile. Discreet blackboards advertise its existence; otherwise a quiz relies entirely on word of mouth, which is unfortunate, because no one talks about it. Oh, obviously you and I and others talk about it non-stop and at maximum volume should we happen to have won this week. We give our loved ones a question-by-question rundown until they fall asleep, or their breathing becomes laboured. But we rarely refer to the subject beyond our immediate circle. Onion-like layers of embarrassment enshroud our secret. We think outsiders would not understand. We are right: they probably wouldn't. Accordingly quizzing has become the silent sub-culture, possibly the only one left that dares not speak its name.

Even if you discount natural British reserve, there are sound reasons for this. Pub quizzes suffer from what marketing men sitting behind hardboard desks in glass hutches on the fourth floors of giant corporate HQs in Maidenhead and Reading would call 'an image problem'. Words like 'anorak' are commonly bandied about, for this is not a glamorous pursuit. Naomi Campbell and Giorgio Armani are rarely seen in my local pub, the Prince of Wales, although someone from *The Bill* has been known to drop by. Trend-spotting magazines and newspapers pay us little attention. (On second thoughts this may be just as well. Some of the quizzing knitwear I have seen over the years needs no further publicity.) For all sorts of fundamental reasons quizzing will never be fashionable. In the hierarchy of hipness we look up to supermodels, fashion designers and trip-hop sound collectives from Bristol, and we look down on people who wear *Star Trek* uniforms in their spare time. This is our lot in life, and we accept it.

For quizzing is not a dignified pastime. If it weren't bad enough sitting around a small table filling in answer sheets – echoes of teenage exam horror are impossible to dispel – there are the behaviour patterns that even the humblest pub quiz seems to generate. This passion to compete does odd things to the brain's chemistry. Polite, amiable people become aggressive and voluble, while those of us already blessed with forceful natures become drooling, barking monsters. All the frustrations of the day are forgotten for a few hours – but in the process, all the emotions that have been repressed come pouring out, simply because you can't remember which Roman Road ran from London to York.[4] When you awake the following morning you are amazed your knuckles are not raw and bleeding.

---

[4] Ermine Street.

After all, they had been dragging along the floor most of the previous evening.

Sometimes you want to win so much your eyes nearly pop out. Being British, of course, we all pretend we are taking part for the sake of taking part, but everyone knows that that went out with long trousers at Wimbledon. It's the sort of buzz top-level professional sportsmen experience all the time. Sadly, few of us are top-level professional sportsmen. All we have are our large, fact-packed brains, distended by years of miscellaneous schooling. Unfortunately we live in possibly the only country in the world which disapproves of outward signs of braininess. Only in the English language is there the phrase 'too clever by half'. We have always preferred the slightly dim amateur, the plucky failure, the bespectacled halfwit whose ski-jumps are measured in centimetres rather than metres.

Within these skulls, our oversized brains throb with frustration. We know the only two South American countries that are landlocked.[5] But what is the use of such a fact unless we can share it with others? All the knowledge in the world is worthless if you can't display it in front of your friends and rivals. Showing off is a natural human impulse. Only a lucky few can run multinational companies or appear regularly on Radio 4. The rest of us must find an alternative means of expression. The pub quiz is heaven-sent.

We all need to play. 'All work and no play makes Jack a dull boy,' as our parents used to tell us when they wanted us to go away and leave them alone. These days, all work and no play makes Jack a snarling psychopath who screams at drivers on motorways and conducts a fumbling affair with his secretary. Adult life has become so unforgiving, so weighed down with responsibility, that we are apt to forget our need to play,

---

[5] Bolivia and Paraguay.

or at least underestimate its importance. Here the pub quiz comes into its own, providing hard-fought competition that manages to be both deadly serious and completely meaningless. You also see your friends and drink lots of nice nourishing beer.

It may be that we are so used to being sold things, to being told that what we haven't is better than what we have, that what comes from abroad is more desirable than what originates here, that when something as simple and unpretentious and innately British as the pub quiz comes along, we don't know what to do with it. There's no money to be made from it. There are no commercial spin-offs. No one does it because it's cool. We do it because a pub quiz is a licence to grown-ups to play and show off and behave like vile know-all children prone to sulks and violent mood swings – all at negligible expense and without fear of public disclosure. Here is that inner child of whom psychiatrists speak. Only in this case it's the inner swot.

This book is an attempt to make sense of it all. It asks the right questions and, more pertinently, answers them, offering occasional bonus points to check that you have been paying attention. It delves back into quizzing history (should we have opened the box, or taken the money?). It marvels at the world-wide phenomenon that was Trivial Pursuit, and wishes it had thought of it first. It puts *Fifteen-To-One* on the timer, and switches on the answering machine during *University Challenge*. And it supplies loads of smart aleck questions for you to steal when you come to set your own quiz – which you will, if you haven't done so already. For once you have succumbed to the lure of quiz, you can never break free. Ask 'Nick'. Just don't mention my name.

2
Quiz

'The brain that doesn't feed itself, eats itself.'

(Gore Vidal)

Somewhere around 1780 – no one is sure of the precise date, or whether any of this happened at all – a Dublin theatre manager named Daly laid a small wager. Within twenty-four hours, he said, he could introduce into the language a word that had absolutely no meaning whatsoever. We don't know who accepted his wager, but whoever it was cannot have known about the large consignment of paint Mr Daly obviously had salted away for the purpose. For overnight the word 'quiz' came to be daubed on almost every prominent wall in the city. Dubliners were intrigued. What could it mean? By tea-time the curious monosyllable was on everyone's lips. Accordingly, Mr Daly won his bet and the word entered the language, suitably defined as a person who banters or chaffs another. The poor fool who lost the bet presumably felt well and truly quizzed.

Words rarely stay in one place for long, and soon any odd or eccentric person was being called a quiz. On 24 June 1782, a bright summer's day tempered by a fresh easterly wind,

Madame d'Arblay wrote in her diary, 'He's a droll quiz, and I rather like him.' Sixteen years later in *Northanger Abbey* Jane Austen wrote: 'Where did you get that quiz of a hat?' As yet there was no direct reference to tie-breakers or 'scores on the doors', but the word mutated again in the early 19th century, when it came to mean a practical joke, a hoax or a piece of humbug. Sir Walter Scott in 1810: 'I am impatient to know if the whole be not one grand blunder or quiz.' Nearly two hundred years later, thousands of failed contestants on *Fifteen-To-One* would know exactly how he felt.

It was not until 1867 that the modern meaning of 'quiz' finally asserted itself. On 26 December of that year (brisk northerly breeze, scattered showers dying out later) the American philosopher and psychologist William James offered the following sage advice to a colleague: 'Occasional review articles, etc., perhaps giving "quizzes" in anatomy and physiology . . . may help you along.' The modern reader will be struck by his slightly tentative use of inverted commas, which may have been brought on by an excess of Christmas pudding. And yet by the end of the century, all the word's previous meanings had fallen into disuse. William James, incidentally, was the elder brother of the novelist Henry James. How he would have marvelled that, just 130 years later, so many people would know his sibling's name as the answer to a quiz question, without having read or having any intention of reading his notoriously indigestible books.

The concept of quizzing, of course, long predates the word. Ever since man could read and write, he has been compelling others to sit down and answer questions on subjects they know nothing about. The main problem in the early years of education was that there wasn't much to know, and most people didn't know it anyway. For several centuries they filled in with riddles, which exercised the minds of the intelligent but idle in much the same way that *The Times* crossword does today.

The Venerable Bede, also destined to become a regular quiz answer, was an especially enthusiastic riddler, and recorded many for the benefit of his fellow monks. One can imagine the chortles of devoted laughter that echoed through the monasteries of Northumberland whenever the latest Bede rib-tickler started doing the rounds.

The world's first quiz question proper, though, may have been that posed by the Sphinx of Greek mythology. As all schoolboys know, this Sphinx was quite different from the Egyptian sphinx, with the head and breasts of a woman, the body of a dog, the wings of a bird, the paws of a lion and the tail of a serpent. She had a human voice and was thought to be the daughter of Orthos, the two-headed dog of Geryon, presumably because no one else stepped forward to take responsibility. She settled near Thebes, and made her living by setting the inhabitants riddles and eating anyone who could not solve them. The oracles told the Thebans that she would die if anyone could come up with a solution to this particular tie-breaker:

> *What goes on four feet, on two feet, and three,*
> *But the more feet it goes on the weaker it be?*

Generations of optimistic Thebans gave it a try, usually at hours of the day that the Sphinx came to call 'lunchtime' and 'dinnertime'. After decades of zero population growth, a Theban named Oedipus finally hit upon the answer. The creature, he explained, was a man, who crawls on all fours as an infant, walks upright as a grown man, and supports himself with a stick in old age. The Sphinx, her bluff called, threw herself to death from a rock, thus setting an example to anguished quizmasters throughout the ages.

Oedipus can barely have known what he had started, although as he inadvertently married his mother shortly afterwards, he probably did not have much time to dwell on it. Nonetheless, the inclination to quiz seems to have caught on. Plutarch says that Homer died of chagrin when he could not solve a riddle – not a bad story, especially when you consider that almost nothing else is known of Homer at all. Three or four centuries later Plato constructed a long and fruitful philosophical career around a series of question-and-answer sessions which subsequently became known as the Socratic dialogues. 'How can this, that, and the other cat all be one thing – e.g. black?' asks Socrates, who has actually been executed several years before, but no matter. 'Each distinct cat participates in the unique Form of Blackness,' says Plato, who must have the answer sheet hidden under the table. It's a little tame by the standards of the Prince of Wales, but the seeds of quiz culture – and of Western thought – lie within. Socrates, incidentally, later featured prominently in *Bill and Ted's Excellent Adventure*, along with Sigmund Freud, Napoleon Bonaparte, Genghis Khan and Keanu Reeves.

If you are a fundamentalist Christian, and believe that the world was created within 6 days (5.93 according to the latest estimates), you may have different ideas about what constituted the world's first quiz question. In Genesis 2:18, having created the Garden of Eden, and sent Adam in to mow the lawn, the Lord God decides that it is not good for the man to be alone. So from the earth he forms all the wild animals and all the birds of the air. Then he brings them to Adam and – here's the tricky bit – asks him to give them their names. 'No, I've nearly got it,' says Adam, clicking his fingers in frustration. 'Tip of my tongue. Is it an okapi?'

Man gets his own back in Genesis 18 when God is set to destroy Sodom and Gomorrah for general wickedness. Fortunately Abraham is on hand with some tricky teasers. 'Will you really sweep away innocent and wicked together? Suppose there are fifty innocent in the city; will you really sweep it away, and not pardon the place because of the fifty innocent lives?' Hmm, says God, and agrees that if there are fifty such people in Sodom, perhaps he will spare the burning sulphur for the time being. But what if there are forty-five? says Abraham. All right, says God, if there are forty-five I'll spare them. How about forty? says Abraham, with the bit between his teeth. Thus history's first-ever Dutch auction proceeds, centuries before anything will be described as 'Dutch'. You may not consider these to be quiz questions as such, but seasoned quizzers will recognise God's predicament. Those numerical questions really can trip you up. How many England caps did Bobby Charlton win precisely?[1]

Chief quizzer among the disciples, of course, was Simon that shall be called Peter (which upsets everyone called Simon to this day). In Matthew 16 Jesus asks his disciples 'Who do people say the Son of Man is?' (This is the first recorded instance of 'a nice easy one to start'.) 'Some say John the Baptist,' they answer. 'Others say Elijah, others Jeremiah, or one of the prophets.' When in doubt, give a selection of possible answers. You never know, one of them might be right.

Jesus, though, remains a step ahead. 'And you?' he asks them. 'Who do you say I am?' A nasty one, in what, to all intents and purposes, has become an individual round. Only Simon Peter has the answer. 'You are the Messiah, the Son of the living God!' he announces, confident that the points are in the bag. Jesus is delighted. 'Simon son of Jonah, you are favoured indeed!' he cries. 'You did not learn that from any human being; it was revealed to you by my heavenly Father.' The other disciples, of course, are furious. If God had told them too, they would have been able to answer on cue just as

---

[1] 106. Often tragically confused with Bobby Moore's 108.

Simon Peter did. Not only the New Testament's first quiz question, then, but its first cheating scandal as well. You'll notice that when Jesus asks, rather later, 'Why have you forsaken me, Father?', he doesn't get any reply at all.

The historical perspective, though, is always short on answers; instead it just supplies more and more questions. *'Quis custodiet ipsos custodes?'* asked Juvenal around nineteen hundred years ago, to general silence. Or, to quote Samuel Johnson, 'There are innumerable questions to which the inquisitive mind can in this state receive no answer: Why do you and I exist? Why was this world created? Since it was to be created, why was it not created sooner?' Mr Daly, if he existed, if he ever made that bet, and if the word really was 'quiz' and not 'spam' or 'erotomania', can hardly have imagined the consequences of his idle jape. His story does, however, make an excellent quiz question, which is roughly where we came in.

3
Trivia[1]

'What dire offence from am'rous causes springs
What mighty contests rise from trivial things.'

(Alexander Pope)

It is in man's nature to quiz, but only recently has it also been in his diary. If we could be bothered, we could probably trace the origins of quizzing back to the very dawn of civilisation, when dinosaurs roamed the earth and cave paintings turned out to be the bonus round. And yet the quiz culture that now prevails, offering facts laced with hangovers to an ever-growing proportion of the population, is still in its

---

[1] From the Latin *trivium*, meaning 'the junction of three roads'. From this came the adjective *trivialis*, initially defined as 'belonging to the public streets' and so, by extension, 'common'. At some point this must have merged with a later, different use of the root. In medieval learning the trivium was the lower division of the seven liberal arts, consisting of grammar, rhetoric and logic. The higher division, the quadrivium, encompassed arithmetic, astronomy, geometry and music. Perhaps 'quadrivial' should now be resuscitated to mean important, valuable knowledge of a type never required in pub quizzes. Or is this a sufficiently quadrivial definition for it?

infancy. Twenty years ago the pub quiz did not exist. If you had walked into your local to find a man behind a micro-phone reading out general knowledge questions, you would probably have called the police. Pubs were as everyone over forty fondly remembers them: deserted and a bit grimy. Bar billiards was still considered a dangerous innovation, while the 'pub grub' consisted of yesterday's pork pie that someone else had not quite managed to finish.

So if earth's history were compacted into a single calendar year, quiz culture has grown up in the time it takes to put the kettle on. Fortunately everything that happens in the world these days, no matter how fatuous, is documented in exhaus-tive detail. As a result we can trace the provenance of quiz culture back to a single cathartic event, a moment of such divine inspiration that it seems inconceivable that choirs of angels were not on hand to witness it. Or TV crews, which shows how much else has changed since then.

In 1979 in Montreal, two journalists with enormous mous-taches were playing Scrabble. Details of the game have never been released, but it seems reasonable to assume that someone else had just put down AXOLOTL on a triple-word square, as someone else always does. It is at moments like these that so many of us decide that Scrabble is not the game for us, and that we do not care whether 'oont' is an Anglo-Indian dialect term for camel, or not. But whatever the provocation, Scott Abbot and Chris Haney decided that they had had enough of the venerable board game, and they could do something better. With their journalistic training, and luxuriant facial hair, they should be able to devise a workable board-game that would make them multi-millionaires.

It's a common delusion, to which most keen board-game players succumb from time to time. Entranced by the prospect of limitless wealth, you waste months fiddling around with dice and counters and hand-drawn boards, and writing a 150-page rule book no one else will ever read. Finally the prototype is ready. You test it out on friends and relatives, none of whom have the heart to tell you quite how boring it is, or why they are all moving to distant cities and not leaving a forwarding address. But you plug away at it, refining and adjusting, when you should be ripping up and burning, until one day you realise, with a blinding revelation that often presages long-term mental illness, that this may be the most foolish and least efficacious way of making a fast buck ever devised, and that you would be better off selling hard drugs on rundown housing estates, just like everyone else.

Abbot and Haney were the exception that makes a mockery of the rule. Almost alone of board-game ideas over the past forty years, theirs was a winner. With a confidence born of apparently limitless naivety, they formed a holding company with Haney's brother John and set about refining their concept. Crucial to the package were 6,000 general knowledge questions which they researched, wrote and rewrote many times over the next couple of years. They found investors, each of whom stumped up $1,000 for a share of the nascent corporation. Abbot and the Haneys must have been very convincing. Can you imagine stumping up a thousand dollars to underwrite the certain failure of a rotten board-game devised by two Canadians with enormous moustaches? You'd set the dogs on them.

Nonetheless, in May 1982, the first blue boxes of Trivial Pursuit™ appeared in Canadian toy stores. No one gave them an earthly chance. The game broke all the rules. It wasn't a video game, which was about the only sort of game that was selling at the time. It was aimed unequivocally at adults, who had never been known to buy board-games before (although Twister was still doing good business). And it was insultingly expensive. Trivial Pursuit™ (never forget that little ™ mark, because their lawyers certainly don't) initially sold at retail

between $30 and $40, some two or three times the price of
your average box of Totopoly. Wise heads were shaken, and
tuts tutted.

But what do men know of marketing, who only marketing
know? Canadians, having little else to do, went mad for the
new game. Boxes flew off shelves. By Christmas 1982 sales
had surpassed 100,000, in a market where 10,000 would have
constituted a result. A few stray boxes soon found their way
into New York stores, and out of them just as quickly. No
Canadian export since Captain Kirk had made such an
impact. By positioning their game as a 'premium product'
Abbot and Haney had (probably unwittingly) caught the
tenor of the times. 'The backgammon of the '80s,' burbled
one newspaper, forgetting that the backgammon of the '80s
was, in fact, backgammon. New York dinner parties were
instantly awash with trivia. Guests were bolting down their
food, anxious to get on with the real business of the evening.
The *Wall Street Journal* published a fulsome profile of the
moustaches, who were already looking marginally better
groomed. Their company, Horn Abbot, rushed out new ver-
sions of the game to cash in. Silver Screen came in a
luminous silver box, while Sports was an emetic orange. By
November 1983, as the first copies of the British version
crept into a few expensive London stores, sales in the US and
Canada were approaching three and a half million. What is
the plural of mongoose? Do mosquitoes have teeth? Over the
next few years we would hear these and other questions
again and again, and come to regret that we had ever heard
the words 'Trivial' or 'Pursuit'.[2]

There were no doubt excellent marketing reasons for the

---

[2] The plural of mongoose is 'mongooses'. Mosquitoes do have teeth,
albeit very small ones.

worldwide success of Trivial Pursuit. It was the right product (flash, overpriced) for the right time. It was cleverly designed and skilfully promoted, rendered fashionable by artful PR manipulation and buckets of well-matured bullshit. Unfortunately, as a game, which after all was its primary function, Trivial Pursuit was a bit of a pudding. Which, at dinner parties, was also what it tended to replace, to the frustration and disappointment of the greedier guests.

The game's primary flaw was its randomness. Some players could wander the board for several days without getting a sniff of a 'cheese' square, while others picked up three or four cheeses in one go. In time most players became skilled at jumping between the Throw Again squares, answering as few questions as possible and loitering within range of the required cheese square until luck turned their way. Any game that uses dice depends to some extent on good fortune, but with Trivial Pursuit a game could be over before it had started if someone was on a roll. Or to be precise, a game could be over before *you* had started, which wasn't on at all. We all wanted to win Trivial Pursuit, and a few people almost expected to. And someone who knew nothing about anything usually managed to instead.

So, by a strange process of social osmosis, it gradually became accepted that the game was crap but the questions were the thing. People would say, 'Let's junk the game and just ask each other the questions.' Cheeses ceased to matter, as did the argument over whether they should be called cheeses or cakes. (If the little things were cakes, what was the big round thing you put them in? The big cake?) Quiz culture, barely extant, was already beginning to evolve.

Then, suddenly, we knew all the questions. 'What actor has "Scotland Forever" tattooed on his right arm?' Yeah, yeah, yeah, that's Sean Connery. 'What did James I do to a loin of beef to make it a sirloin of beef?' Knighted it. Were there any

we hadn't heard before? Knowing the questions gave you an
advantage, but not a very satisfying one. On the whole you
would just have preferred new questions. And if there were
going to be new questions, for God's sake make them better
questions. What you didn't know was that the British version
of Trivial Pursuit had been written in a tearing hurry by a
couple of blokes Abbot and the Haneys had met on holiday in
Spain. Ray Loud ran a fine art business and Steve Birch,
according to the press release of the time, was 'involved in a
bedroom furniture firm'. Professional question-writers they
were not, as became apparent the more you played the game.

Some questions were easy, some were difficult. That's only
as it should be. More than a few, though, were impossible. A
lot were dull. A fair number were simply wrong. (Q: 'What is
a nanosecond?' A: 'A millionth of a second.') Most irritating of
all, perhaps, were the questions that didn't really mean anything. 'What is London's most famous bookshop?' You would
probably say Foyles, but if you had said Dillons, who was to
say that you were wrong?

In most households the big blue box eventually gravitated
to the top of a cupboard, where it languishes today. You don't
chuck away a Trivial Pursuit: it's too pleasing an artefact for
that. But nor do you open it, let alone play it, from one year
to the next. Somehow it wouldn't seem appropriate. It's as
much of its time as the footballer's fluffy haircut, or Sir
Norman Fowler.

And yet its influence was far-reaching. Trivial Pursuit was
the onlie begetter of today's quiz culture: schoolgirl mother,
absent father, judgmental grandparent and ill-informed social
worker all rolled into one. We may not have known what it
was called. (Ten years later, four out of five pensioners tripped
over in the street still insist on calling it 'Trivial Pursuits'.) We
may have been unable to take the cheese out of the cake (or
the little cake out of the big cake) without a Swiss Army

knife. We may have been driven insane by the constant use of 'What' at the start of a question, when human beings would have said 'Which'. But in the process we discovered something about ourselves we did not know was there. Something deep within our psyches, something primevally swotty, responded to the call of these questions. Which is the only mammal that can't jump?[3] What was Ted Kennedy convicted of in the Chappaquiddick accident?[4] Which London theatre boasted the legend 'We never closed,' until it did?[5]

Once you had exhausted these questions, the natural response was to look around and ask, what's next? Between us, my friends and I bought several Trivial Pursuit-like games, all cruelly expensive and packaged in unnecessarily impressive boxes. Pictionary was the drawing one, Balderdash was the lying one and Outburst, much the best of the lot, was the shouting one, but eventually the primeval urge to answer quiz questions overwhelmed all other considerations. In 1987 my old college friend Terence threw a dinner party in the week between Christmas and New Year, and asked me if I would prepare a brief quiz to keep his guests conscious while his rather weighty food churned through their digestive systems. An interesting challenge, I thought, little realising that I would be producing such quizzes for his post-Yuletide meals for what is now beginning to look like the rest of my life.

Trivial Pursuit's commercial peak, meanwhile, is long past. The game still sells in comfortable quantities, although Hasbro, who manufacture the game under licence in the UK, are strikingly reluctant to reveal how comfortable those quantities are,

---

[3] The elephant.
[4] Leaving the scene of an accident.
[5] The Windmill.

or indeed anything about the game at all. But Trivial Pursuit has done its job. Quiz culture is up and running, out of copyright, beyond the reach of lawyers, and with no royalties payable to anyone. This may be its most satisfying legacy of all.

4
People and Places

'War in the old days made men. *We have not the same sterling times to live in and must look for other outlets for our energy.'*

(Ernest Shackleton)

As the allure of Trivial Pursuit faded in 1986, natural-born quizzers began to look around for new ways to show off their burgeoning general knowledge. At around the same time, manufacturers of video games were seeking to expand beyond their traditional strongholds (seedy amusement arcades, student beer cellars) and tap into a new and potentially lucrative market of sad drunk men in pubs with nothing better to do.

And so the trivia machine was born.

You could call it serendipity. You could call it coincidence. Over the subsequent year or so, more than a few quizheads would come to call it extra unearned income, as they toured the country emptying these machines of their takings. My friend Chris says he quickly 'discovered a facility' for them. With a partner-in-quiz he would spend most Friday and Saturday evenings working the pubs of north London, answering the same questions many times over and generally cleaning up. 'Go in, two halves of lager, ten minutes, fifty quid and out the door,' was the almost romantic way he described it to the

rest of us much later. We thought armed robbers would consider that a fair rate of return. 'The theory was that other
people put the money in during the week, and we took it out
at weekends.' Their largest haul from a single machine was
£85, their best evening produced £200, and over about six
months they pocketed just over £3,000.

Oddly enough, almost everyone I have asked about this has
a similar story to tell. One fellow I know claims to have emptied most of the machines in Yorkshire, while another cut a
swathe across the whole south-west of England. Another
couple concentrated solely on motorway service stations in an
attempt to reduce their mountainous student debts. George
Soros personally accounted for all the quiz machines in
Glasgow, while Bill Gates annexed wide areas of Lancashire. I
was at the Roxy in 1976 on the night the Sex Pistols formed,
and Lloyd George knew your father.

Nonetheless, those early machines were famously easy.
Variously known as Triv Quiz, Trivia Quiz, Quiz-u-lator and
about five hundred other titles, these pioneering consoles gave
you a choice of six subjects (People and Places, Pot Luck,
Entertainment, Sport, Pop and General Knowledge) and asked
you to answer a simple multiple-choice question – press A, B
or C – before the time ran out. As an idea it was unbeatable:
today most trivia machines still use the same basic format. But
the weeny computer memories of 1986 – a year in which the
bestselling home computer was the Sinclair 48K Spectrum –
limited the database to around 5,000 questions: half the
number of Trivial Pursuit. In practice you only had to play a
quiz machine four or five times before familiar questions
started to reappear. Even if you didn't know the answers when
you started, you soon would. Another problem was the prolif-
eration of blatantly wrong answers on the database. Players
encountering these errors for the first time could be forgiven
for smashing in the console's screen with a sledgehammer.

After a few games, though, you came to know the machine's tricks. You could deal with the random misspellings, and the questions that relied on value-judgement rather than immutable fact. For once you had the machine's number, you usually had its money. Unless, of course, someone else had had its money first.

It took the manufacturers about six months to realise the extent to which they had cocked up. It wasn't just the brainy obsessives who were clearing them out. Even drunks at the end of a hard evening's rambling and belching were winning their money back, and no pub landlord likes to see that. There had to be new questions, and they had to be much harder.

A new database was constructed. This second wave of questions recognised what the manufacturers should have worked out a long time before: that if men in pubs know about anything, it's about pop music and sport. They may be a little fallible on mountain ranges or pre-20th century Prime Ministers, but they know who recorded 'In the Year 2525'[1] and how many football teams won the League Championship in the 1980s[2]. In the second wave, then, such questions were substantially beefed up. Casual punters carried on putting the money in, and were often too drunk to realise that they were no longer taking it out.

The brainy obsessives, meanwhile, continued much as before. They recognised that they would have to work harder for their winnings, but they were happy to do so. Fortunately, the new database had not supplanted the old one overnight. There were still a few machines to be found that offered the same old questions, and the same old payouts. If you did track

---

[1] Zager and Evans.
[2] Four (Aston Villa and Arsenal once each, Everton twice and Liverpool the other six times).

one of these down, you fell upon it with unabashed delight.
But as the old database was phased out, obsessives worked to
master the new questions. Soon they were emptying machines
again with all their old skill. There were fewer factual errors
in the new questions, which showed signs of having been put
together with care. But the time you were given to answer
each question had been drastically reduced. As the cash prizes
grew nearer, you barely had a second to react. Here was a
challenge no competitive male could resist.

For two or three years in the late 1980s, wherever men and
women would gather together, men would play the quiz
machine and women, well, wouldn't. Dartboards lay unused,
and the holes on pool tables began to heal up. One man, usually the one who had invested the money (but not always),
would press the buttons, while the others stood around shouting the answers, often incoherently. No one was less popular
than the man who knew nothing but thought he knew everything, and shouted the loudest. Over time a certain
intellectual hierarchy would assert itself, with the brainiest
edging closer to the front and the action. As the games
became more complex, and the questions harder, much less
money was won than it had been before. But more people had
much more fun.

The most popular trivia machine of the period, and possibly of any period, was Give Us a Break. These days it's hard
to imagine that the Radio 1 DJ Dave Lee Travis had any lasting influence on British culture, but if he did have, this was it.
Give Us a Break began as a quiz insert on his tattifilarious
Sunday lunchtime show, embodying the chortlesome notion of
'snooker on the radio'. Paul Daniels had already performed
card tricks on the radio, and decades earlier Peter Brough and
Archie Andrews had taken ventriloquism on the radio to new
heights. The Hairy Cornflake, whose sense of humour was
legendary (or non-existent, depending on your point of view),

chose to exploit snooker's brief bubble of popularity with a weekly phone-in quiz, which he conducted, chewing furiously on his pipe, between records by Queen and ELO. Possibly unwittingly, he had created the template for the most memorable of all pub trivia machines, a game that would continue to be played long after DLT himself had stomped out of Radio 1 and began a bright new career in local radio. As a disc jockey his legacy is hard to define, but his place in the pantheon of quiz greats is assured.

On radio, and in pubs, the game worked in the same straightforward manner. A red ball was an easy question for one point. Get that right and you could choose a colour: a yellow for two, a green for three, up to a black for seven. The higher the value, the harder the question, and on the trivia machine, the less time you had to answer it. You would build a break in the normal way, amassing points which you hoped would turn into prizes. Ingeniously, the size of the prizes was determined by how much money had been deposited in the machine by others before your arrival. So if no one had won for a while, the game was rich pickings, with £1 to be won barely before you knew it, and the top prize of £10 easily accessible to the more ambitious players. Once you had won, the points needed to win again were immediately hiked up, thus deterring brainy obsessives from reducing the machine's profit margin further. Which meant, of course, that you tried just that, conscious that if you lost a couple of times, it didn't matter, as the big prizes would again be in reach.

Give Us a Break ended all male conversation in pubs for at least a year. Fruit machines are a solitary vice (and as expensive as most of the others). Other pub games are at best a temporary distraction. Give Us a Break, on the other hand, could keep a group of men entertained for an entire evening. It could also keep them drinking for an entire evening. The satisfying little buzz of adrenalin the game generated both accelerated alcohol consumption and appeared to delay its effects. (Often you only knew how drunk you had been when you woke up the following morning.) Pub landlords smiled upon their money-spinner, and positioned it prominently. In the minds of some of them, ideas for an even cheaper way of making money out of quizmania began to seed.

Like so many crazes Give Us a Break soon became a victim of its own popularity. So many people were playing the game, and playing it well, that the questions had to be made even harder, the time limit even shorter. Other, more sophisticated trivia machines were developed to rival the market leader, but they didn't play as well, or they were too expensive, or just too difficult. Gradually men filtered back to the pool table. Some even started talking to their girlfriends again. By late 1991, when I found myself going to the Cock Tavern in Great Portland Street every Monday evening with a group of fellow writers, the era of the quiz machine had passed. The pub still had one, hiding in a corner, and we still played it, but only after the proper quiz had finished in the lounge bar upstairs. Possibly for the first time in technological history, man was replacing machine. People now sought the human touch. Quiz culture was evolving again.

That Cock Tavern quiz, which we chanced upon one night and, as is the way of these things, returned to again and again like moths to a floodlight, was run by the pub's landlord, a weary Scotsman known (after a character in *Viz*) as Billy Quiz. Most pubs in the West End of London are dedicated to fleecing tourists and drunken officeworkers; they don't need the extra revenue that a quiz would generate, and they certainly don't need the workload. Billy Quiz, however, was an enthusiast, armed with a modest library of reference books and a thorough knowledge of Scottish lower league football. By later standards his quiz wasn't especially entertaining or imaginative, but it was the only one around, and it was our first experience of the form. We were quiz virgins.

My quizmates at the Cock Tavern were comedy writers, and therefore all poor, grumpy and fantastically competitive. It takes a certain temperament to write jokes for a living. Most comedy writers are bitter, furious men who cannot believe that their huge talent has not yet been transformed into vast sums of money. Years after our Cock Tavern phase, one of our team did indeed strike it rich, and now lives in an enormous house to which he rarely invites the rest of us. The others are as angry and impoverished as ever.

I am not surprised that they are so cross: they are all very bright. Each has the sort of broad and incisive intelligence that is perfectly suited to the rigours of the pub quiz, if not to making enough money to live. Of our number, Michael knew everything about the natural world, and a lot about everything else. Mark knew more about American culture than anyone who lived in Hammersmith really ought to, while Simon and Ged were both expert in football and pop music, among several other subjects. In such august company I was strictly a makeweight. We tended to win, on average, every other week, which made us deeply popular with all the other regulars. Simon was our secret weapon. His in-depth knowledge of Scottish lower league football secured most of our more convincing victories. When he wasn't there we tended to come fifth. Only one team consistently threatened us, a group of four odd-looking men in suits. After they had trounced us one week, we discussed their physical appearance at some length and decided, a little cruelly, that they would have had a hard time finding girlfriends. So we christened them 'the Quiz Virgins'.

Such low levels of banter, and the fact that the prizes were all measured in pints of beer, kept us in Tuesday morning hangovers for six happy months. Then Billy Quiz, whose talents had obviously been recognised by head office, was sent off to rescue some doomed boozer in Scunthorpe or Slough, and the Cock Tavern quiz came to an end.

We looked around for a West End replacement, but never found one. Instead, with a convert's zeal, I began to investigate the pubs near my home in North London. Here quizzes were quietly spawning. A group of us, all regulars at Terence's annual Christmas quizzes, sampled half a dozen or so, and after a few false starts, found The Wrestlers, an old man's pub on the lower slopes of Highgate Hill. It was not the most promising location. Decorated in the style of your grandparents, and steeped in quiet desperation, The Wrestlers was one of those pubs whose continued existence could only be ascribed to an accounting error. At the bar sat silent pensioners who could make half of lager last as long as my childhood. A tape of Tom Petty and the Heartbreakers' 'Full Moon Fever' played over and over again. The landlord was friendly enough, though apparently unaware that there were any crisp flavours other than ready salted. A strange barman called Brendan winked ominously every time you went to buy a drink. Occasionally passers-by would walk in, look around and walk quickly out again. Even the gents' lavatory was more fragrant than some of the customers.

Just about the only thing the pub had going for it, in fact, was Chris and Barry's Monday night quiz. For one night only the pub was heaving. Tables that lay empty for the rest of the week now had to be claimed at least half an hour before kick-off. The Milkmen (as one team were known, as they were indeed milkmen) drove in each week from Stoke Newington. Bachelor teachers from the nearby school sat in one corner and exchanged obscure geographical facts. A team of (we guessed) estate agents twitched by the bar. The Wrestlers, in short, felt like a good place to be. Even the pensioners at the bar seemed to perk up. I distinctly remember one of them buying a pint.

For Chris and Barry's quiz was a good quiz: expertly crafted, challenging and conveniently tailored to our own areas of expertise. Without my comedy-writing friend Simon, we had no cause to regret our ignorance of Scottish football or the more abstruse corners of current pop activity (another Billy Quiz speciality) – although Chris and Barry were a little too keen on horse racing for our tastes, and they became even keener when they discovered how little we all knew about it.

Also keener was the competition. Of several brain-packed teams who came and went during our two-year stint at The Wrestlers, our bitterest rivals were a team led by a short, bald Scotsman in his thirties named George. Unsmiling, and forever dressed in black, George appeared to know everything. He was also a fearsome competitor, who was as determined to beat us as we were to beat him. There was the added incentive that his team seemed much cooler than we were. For a few weeks they even included the pop star Feargal Sharkey, which represented a masterpiece of team selection by any standards. 'Is that Feargal Sharkey?' we wondered. 'In The Wrestlers?' Well, yes it was, although such was the nature of the place that virtually no one else noticed him. They would probably have known him as the answer to a quiz question long before they recognised his face.

Chris and Barry presided over this with quiet dignity and a fair amount of free lager. Chris (mid-forties, bearded, bald, mellow, bit of an old hippy at heart) read out the questions, while Barry (same age, droopy moustache, even more of an old hippy) sat back and smoked roll-ups. This was the only quiz they delivered personally, but they wrote weekly quizzes for several pubs in North London as a hobby, which they hoped would one day become more than a hobby and make them rich. Missing the company of my comedy-writing friends, I immediately latched on to this blind and deluded optimism. After the quiz was done we would hang around talking and drinking until the landlord threw us out. In our various ways we are all diffident souls, and it took several years for these friendships to coalesce. But what men may lack in social skills, they make up for in the sheer quantity of rubbish they have to discuss. We always had Chris and Barry's questions to rip apart, and Chris and Barry, in turn, mocked our inability to answer them. Long-standing friendships were quietly formed on those strange Mondays, as Brendan stood behind the bar winking and we all wondered what was wrong with him.

The Wrestlers' quiz had its time, and then ended. A new landlord arrived, determined to spruce up the old place and fill it with striving young quantity surveyors with eye-watering after-shave and mobile phones. The pensioners drifted away, and oddly enough so did everyone else. Fewer and fewer teams turned up on Mondays, and you could see the new landlord blamed Chris and Barry for this. The pub was then renamed The Slug and Lettuce, which repelled most remaining customers. It was time to move on. So, with a farewell wave to the Milkmen (who had remained loyal to the last), Chris and Barry resigned their quizmasterly activities, and left the pub for ever. (Or at least until the following week, when they popped in for a drink.)[3]

Once again we had been rendered quizless. No doubt we cut sorry figures over those weeks, scouring the pubs of North London to find a replacement. The Wrestlers, for all its faults, had been our territory: we knew the best tables to sit at, and which bar snacks should be buried in concrete ten miles under the earth's surface. Now, whichever pub we visited, we were the outsiders. Pub-goers look strangely at outsiders at the best

---

[3] The Slug and Lettuce was so successful in its new incarnation that it was quickly renamed 'The Slug and Lettuce at the Wrestlers'. Nowadays it's 'The Wrestlers' again, and all the pensioners are back on their stools as though the 1990s never happened.

of times. When outsiders then win the quiz, it's not the best of times. At a terrifying old pub near Alexandra Palace, we seriously thought we were going to be beaten up. We had only won £18, but by doing so we had obviously transgressed some unwritten law of pub etiquette. Middle-aged women with towering hairdos looked down their noses at us, while the bar staff were embarrassed even to serve us. Perhaps by pouring our drinks they too risked personal harm. Only Terence, who never notices his surroundings, was unaware of the potential peril. When we left, no doubt he wondered why we all sprinted for our cars.

Eventually we settled at another Highgate pub, the Prince of Wales, where we remain to this day. In the intervening years team members have come and gone. Two of our number have moved out of London, although David still drives down from Oxfordshire every six weeks or so, seventy miles here, seventy miles back, with three pints of diet Coke in between. He thinks it's worth it. We laugh at his zeal, but we think it's worth it, too. Terence and I are still regulars, as is Chris, our former quizmaster at The Wrestlers, and George, our former bitter rival. (Of Feargal Sharkey nothing was ever heard again.) There are others who join us more occasionally, of whom more later. Each Tuesday night we can be found in one of the pub's shadier corners, crouched around a small table, arguing. Is it Boyle's Law or Charles's Law? Sheffield United or Sheffield Wednesday? If we knew, we wouldn't be arguing. But then if we weren't arguing, we probably wouldn't be there.

5
The Prince of Wales

'Gently my eyelids close;
I'd rather be good than clever;
And I'd rather have my facts all wrong
Than have no facts whatever.'

(Ogden Nash)

Let us set the scene. It is Tuesday night, at around 8:30. The Prince of Wales is quiet tonight, which is to say deafeningly loud by normal standards, for in this tiniest of pubs one is company and two's a crowd. Tall people are discouraged by its low ceilings, while fatties struggle to negotiate its unforgiving doors. But the regulars love it. While a stool remains unoccupied, and the lungs can still extract the occasional molecule of oxygen from the cigarette smoke, most of us would not go anywhere else. You may wonder why a pub of such distinctive charm and meagre proportions should feel it necessary to run a weekly quiz to boost takings. Several customers, who have no desire to take part in anything remotely resembling a quiz, will be wondering this in around half an hour's time. For the marketing men at the brewery, though, no pub can be too busy. Only when the Prince of Wales is indistinguishable from the Tokyo underground at rush hour will they be satisfied.

For the moment, though, normal business conditions apply.

In winter a fire so realistic it can only be powered by gas will be roaring in the hearth. Anyone standing within ten feet will be wondering where that smell of singed flesh is coming from. In summer, eddies of concentrated body heat will be maintaining an ambient temperature equivalent to Gas Mark 4. The pub knows no seasons, and the seasons know no change. By 8:30, whatever the time of year, most of the after-work drinkers will be starting to drift away, mindful of other commitments. A hard core, shabbier and more determined than the rest, will be settling in for the long haul. One or two teachers from the nearby school will be particularly well established: no homework for them tonight. In a corner an adulterous couple will be congratulating themselves on having discovered such a cosy, unassuming little pub, where no one will recognise them. They will have failed to notice the large blackboard positioned prominently above their furtive embraces, announcing in multi-coloured chalk that the weekly quiz will begin at 9 o'clock.

Between 8:30 and 9:00 a subtle change comes over the pub. As non-quizzers wander off, so quizzers gradually replace them, sidling through the front door as though they just happened to be passing and thought they might look in. This is a pose that lasts as long as it takes to adjust your vision to the pub's customary murk. Most of us are barely halfway to the bar before we are peering around, trying to see who else has turned up. Many of the same old faces will already be there, eyeing each other with suspicion. Acknowledge them as you see them, maybe with a nod, or even a small, slightly bitter smirk. 'Here we are again,' such a smirk will say, 'and by remaining cool I can pretend to myself that I really have something much more sensible to do this evening, although obviously I don't.'

In reality, it's quite comforting to see the same old faces week after week, much as we might pretend otherwise. The

same old faces in the same old pub, with the same modest aim
in mind: to win tonight's top prize of £13.50 and be glared at
by all the other teams who don't. You recognise the faces even
though you may not yet know the names, or have long since
forgotten them. Most are looking for their team-mates, and at
the same time identifying and evaluating their potential opponents. It's all very polite and gentlemanly, with a subtext of
pure aggression.

Slowly, then, the tenor of the evening alters. Where quizzers
will gather, the conversation is bound to turn to the important
issues of the day, such as Division Three scoring records and
the name of the Secretary of State for Social Security. In fact,
not that many Prince of Wales quizzers come in here during
the rest of the week, unless they have won the £10 drinks'
voucher in the bonus round. This is an ingenious wheeze by
the pub, as the voucher expires at the end of business on the
following Sunday. If you want to use the voucher, you can
either slurp up dangerously quickly the same evening – usually a waste of your prize, as everyone is well on the way
already – or you can come back later in the week for a cele-
bratory drink, during which far more than £10 will be spent.
This is because only a few regular Prince quizzers live near
enough to use the pub as a local. Most of us make a special
journey to come here, so if we make two special journeys a
week instead of one, we are likely to spend a lot more money.
We come to the Prince on Tuesdays because the quiz is the
best in the area: it's as simple as that.

Genuine regulars view the influx with a combination of
alarm and contempt. 'Who are these people?' says one old
bloke every Tuesday, although you would have thought he
had worked it out by now. Man is a territorial animal, and
pub-going man has failed to shake off any of his more primi-
tive instincts. He protects his bar stool as a Neanderthal guards
his cave, albeit with marginally less success. Neanderthal Man

would growl, jump about and throw sharp implements at his assailant. Pub-Going Man merely gives you a good glare, and if really roused, say 'I don't know what the world is coming to.' No one pays him any attention.

As quiz hour approaches, the scramble for tables grows more intense. There is always one little man who has secured the largest and most comfortable table in the pub, and proceeds to spread out most of his belongings to discourage anyone else from sitting there. Opening broadsheet newspapers across the table, draping jackets over every chair, skilfully dumping his briefcase where most people will trip over it, he will repel all attacks and nurse a half of cider till his friends finally roll in. 'Is this seat taken?' ask at least twenty people. 'Oh yes,' says Early Bird, unable to keep a tone of mild censure out of his voice. If you wanted to sit down, you should have arrived earlier.

The rest of us must try to identify groups of people who have found tables but may be about to leave shortly. This is a delicate matter, because they may not yet know that they are about to leave. They sit in innocent comfort, exchanging tittle-tattle and idly plotting the downfall of colleagues at work. They may just have bought another round. They don't intend to vacate their seats for a while yet. They glance up at us, clearly mystified. Why do we loiter so? What on earth gives us the impression that they may soon be on their way?

Shortly, though, the microphone will be plugged in and this week's quizmaster will say, 'Good evening, and welcome to the Prince of Wales's Tuesday night quiz.' Within seconds tables will magically become available. Regulars are resigned to the existence of the quiz, and the adulterous couple in the corner won't even notice, but many ordinary punters, who had been enjoying what they thought was a quiet drink, will drain their glasses with a gulp and run screaming for the door. Some won't slow down until they reach home. They may well know the name of the President of Estonia, but on this occasion they would prefer to keep such knowledge to themselves.

It is essential, therefore, to identify which punters will flee and which will say yeah, why not, let's stay and have a go. All regular teams like to think they have a nose for this. Most have spent whole months of Tuesdays looming over occupied tables, trying to be menacing in the politest possible way, and willing the incumbents to leave. But there's no way of knowing for sure. Sometimes it works, sometimes it doesn't. And the stakes are high. You could secure the most comfortable table in the pub. Or if they decide to stay, you could have wasted anything up to half an hour's valuable looming time. This could prove decisive, for on a busy evening you might have to endure what to many is the ultimate quizzing disaster: being forced to stand. Where do you put your drinks? How can you huddle effectively to discuss the questions and agree that the quizmaster is an idiot? Clinical tests show that a quizzer's concentration and intellectual acuity are liable to suffer if he is denied access to a comfortable chair.

Eventually the quizmaster arrives, holding a sheaf of papers covered with scribbles. He is barely able to contain his excitement. As Jeremy Paxman has discovered, there are few roles in adult life more delicious than that of quizmaster. In the Prince of Wales we take turns to set and read out the quiz, and I think we all know which is the better half of the deal. Setting questions involves hard toil, even if you steal them all from quiz books or *Fifteen-To-One*. Reading them out requires only a couple of stiff drinks for Dutch courage. After that you are away, surfing on a tide of ego and power. No wonder William G Stewart does it every day.

One important perk the quizmaster enjoys is his own table. No hanging about for him, waiting for non-quizzers to leave. In most pubs the quizmaster's table will be set aside for the grand ritual. It may be the most prominently positioned table available, or just the nearest to the appropriate electrical sockets, but it is the quizmaster's territory and so out of bounds to all lesser beings. This category includes the four big blokes who are currently sitting there, having ignored (or possibly removed) the sign saying 'Reserved for Quiz from 8:45 pm'. In normal circumstances the quizmaster would quail from any confrontation with these muscular gentlemen. He is slender and easily crushed, and would probably offer to give them lifts home in his car if they promised not to hit him. Today, however, he is the quizmaster and has the might of right on his side. Smiling superciliously, he asks them to vacate his area. They stare up at him, at his sheaf of papers and his scoring paraphernalia, with infinite contempt. Who does this guy think he is? Then they realise that everyone else is looking at them. Fifty quizzing eyes are scrutinising their narrow foreheads and paleolithic jawlines. Something is going on here that they can have no part of. Suspiciously, reluctantly, they stand up. 'Where else are we supposed to sit?' says one, peevishly. The quizmaster smiles, generous in victory. 'Oh, I think there's another table around the corner.' Not that there is, of course, but he knows that these men are now Someone Else's Problem.

The gorillas leave, usually by the back door, muttering curses. Someone behind the bar switches on the speakers, which emit a stroke-inducing wail of feedback. A man in the process of buying a large round tries to hurry along the bar staff, because he doesn't want to miss any questions. The bar staff serve him even more slowly and deliberately than before. By now, anywhere between seven and sixteen teams are huddled around the Prince's tables, depending on the weather, the football and a thousand other variables of which we can know nothing. There is no justice in this matter. A skilfully wrought quiz, elegantly structured and read with style, wit and grace, may be contested by half-a-dozen teams for a first prize worth less than the bonus-round beer voucher. Similarly quite shoddy quizzes can attract crowds that probably convene all health and safety regulations. It is completely random.

The rules are simple enough. Teams must be no larger than six; the fee is a pound per person; and the top three teams will split the pot in the approximate ratio 3:2:1. There are four rounds in the quiz proper, each of ten questions, plus the bonus round of five questions (for the £10 drinks voucher), which takes place between rounds two and three. (Pay attention: these rules won't be repeated.) Other conventions are less formal, but no less assiduously observed. There will usually be a 'nice easy one to start', which may indeed be a nice easy one, or more probably a villainously difficult one to make the quizmaster feel good about himself. If you are going to let the power go to your head, you may as well do it with question 1.

Then, at the end of each round, we might have 'the scores on the doors'. This phrase is commonly ascribed to Bruce Forsyth, who used it on *The Generation Game* every week for several decades. Why it should have imprinted itself on the memories of every amateur quizmaster in the British Isles is not clear. No one says 'it's good, but it's not right' or 'super smashing great'. But the scores, if they are anywhere in quizland, are invariably on the doors. Such scores, it should be noted, are customarily given 'in no particular order' for the first three rounds, and then 'in reverse order' at the end.

A word on team names. There are two broad schools of thought on this issue, represented by those teams who always use the same name, and those teams who always use different names. The advantages of always using the same name are those of any branded product. Everybody knows who you are, and so everybody is delighted when you do badly. If you start doing well, people may come to respect you, even fear you. If you start doing well too often, people may come to hate your guts. Soon spontaneous boos will greet any mention of your team name. Rival quizmasters will mark your questions unusually harshly. Eventually there may be hints that you find a new quiz in which to show off your undoubted talents. For such teams a strongly branded corporate identity is an obvious hindrance. Far cleverer to travel light.

The main disadvantage of always choosing a different name is that you always have to choose a different name. This can require a titanic intellectual effort after a hard day at work, especially when there are all those drinks to buy, tables to snaffle and opponents to snub. The waggish and topically minded usually like to show off their joke-sculpting skills with a team name that sums up the entire country's current humorous preoccupations in six words, no more than one of which will be 'arse'. Such teams usually come last, exhausted by their self-imposed satirical burden. Go for simplicity every time. Even if you do come up with a formidably clever name, the quizmaster will probably mispronounce it.

Everyone is now settled and ready for action. The man buying the huge round races back to his table with the last few glasses. The bar staff chuckle maliciously. The quizmaster realises that he can delay no longer. He taps the microphone to check that it's working. He clears his throat. He says, 'Round one, question one. Here's a nice easy one to start.'

6
The Knowledge

'It is the tragedy of the world that no one knows what he doesn't know; and the less a man knows, the more sure he is that he knows everything.'

(Joyce Cary)

The first time Russell came to the quiz, he was understandably nervous. 'But I don't know anything,' he pleaded. He didn't actually mean that he didn't know anything, of course. He has an Oxford degree, a flourishing career, an unusually cool flat and a phalanx of beautiful female admirers. He knows enough. What he meant was that he couldn't remember the chemical formula for sulphuric acid or who won the men's Olympic 100 metres in 1984. 'Don't be daft,' I said. 'You'll know far more than you think you know. Everybody does. "General knowledge" is just that: generally known. Somewhere in the musty recesses of your mind, a small voice will be shouting "H_2SO_4! Carl Lewis!" You may be ashamed to remember such rubbish, but remember it you will. Anyway, you haven't got anything else to do this evening.' It was a low blow, and it worked. Russell didn't mind being thought stupid, but to be identified as otherwise unoccupied on a Tuesday night was more than he could bear.

His misapprehension, though, is a common one among non-quizzers. 'But I won't know anything.' Most of us would claim to have had a general knowledge once, before time and neglect and cheap red wine wore it away. Sometimes, during a particularly severe hangover, you believe you can feel the individual brain cells dying. As they perish, it seems only reasonable to assume that individual snippets of information perish with them. The name of the dog in *The Woodentops*. Pop! The scorer of the winning goal in the 1978 FA Cup Final. Pop! Sometimes you can feel whole subjects go. The life and works of Charles Dickens. Pop! Logarithms. Pop! British history 1485–1914. *Pop!*

Except, of course, that the mind doesn't work like that. Brain cells are indeed destroyed in huge numbers by our habitual self-indulgence, but it's only relatively unimportant motor functions that suffer, like walking or how to eat pizza. Ninety per cent of the brain remains uncharted territory, and you can bet that it is somewhere in that 90 per cent that the small voice shouting 'H_2SO_4! Carl Lewis!' has hidden itself. Our general knowledge has not perished, it merely hibernates. All you need are a few quizzes to wake it up.

At his first quiz Russell sat for an hour feeling stupid and redundant, unable even to think of a reasonable excuse to go home. Then, in round three, as brain cell casualties were mounting, a question was asked that only he knew the answer to. This is the blinding light of revelation for most quiz converts, the moment you realise you will be back next week. 'Which European national airline was established in 1919, and remains the oldest surviving international airline to this day?' Blank looks all round, accompanied by sinking hearts, for we had been one point behind the leaders on the last round and every answer counted. 'Lufthansa?' said Chris, on the basis that the Germans are near the front of most important queues and this one would be no exception. Suddenly a gleam appeared in

Russell's eyes – what the rest of us, practised in the art of quiz observation, instantly recognised as the Gleam of Certainty. 'It's KLM,' he announced. We did not argue. We respected the Gleam of Certainty. Needless to say, he was right. That week we won by one point. Russell's answer had been crucial. From that day he was hooked. He had tasted quizzing glory. Now he wanted the full three courses. These days correct answers pour from his well-stocked brain with almost irritating regularity.

Pub quizzes are a skill that can be acquired, or at least resuscitated. Like IQ tests, the more of them you do, the easier they get. When you embark upon a quizzing career, you suspect that if you are ever going to flourish, you are going to have to know things. Other people, sitting around the pub looking clever, already seem to know these things, while the only thing that you know for certain is that you know nothing. What you probably don't know is that you know quite a lot; you just don't know that you don't know that you know it. Once you find out that you never knew how much you know, you will be surprised to find out just how much you know. From there it's just a short step to genuinely knowing things, and even one stage further, thinking you know things while in fact not knowing them at all.

In fact, proper knowledge, in the sense of having seen or experienced something for yourself, is not essential. You do not need to have read all the books or seen all the films. Obviously it helps if you have read all the books, seen all the films and won all the Nobel prizes, because in the quiz world everyone loves a smartarse. But it's not mandatory. More often than not it is less important to have read the book than just to know that it exists. You do not have to have seen *Casablanca* to answer questions on it. You just have to know what sort of questions they are going to ask.

This has led some august commentators to suggest, with

disapproving shakes of the head, that quiz culture is 'shallow'.
That quizzes merely skate across the surface, seeking out
information rather than knowledge and rewarding memory
rather than understanding. This is a plausible analysis, which
could also be applied to the whole of the British education
system. When you are doing O levels or GCSEs you are surprised by how boring the course is and how much
rote-learning it involves. Your teachers assure you A levels
will be much more interesting. When you do A levels, you are
surprised by how boring the course is and how much rote-
learning it involves. Your teachers assure you that your degree
course will be much more interesting. When you read for
your degree, in between hiring out your various orifices to pay
off all the debts you have run up, you are surprised by how
boring the course is and how much rote-learning it involves.
Your tutors assure you that a PhD will be far more interesting,
at which point you run away to join the Foreign Legion or
march into McDonald's with a pump-action shotgun. And they
call quizzes shallow.

It is true that a pub quiz makes few demands on the higher
intellect. It is also rather a relief. If we wandered into the
Prince of Wales on a Tuesday evening and saw Sir Isaiah
Berlin sitting there, we would obviously be very surprised, for
Sir Isaiah is dead. But we would also be relatively unfazed.
One of the huger brains of the 20th century may have resided
in that eminent skull, but his recollection of James Bond theme
tunes was apparently modest. In pub quizzes we are happy to
skate across the surface. We are aware of the icy waters that
lurk threateningly below, and we are determined never to
encounter them if we possibly can. Pub quizzes are shallow,
and so, intellectually at least, are we. We know a little about
a lot, and a lot about very little. We know that beryllium is
number 4 in the periodic table and that it has the chemical
symbol Be. Chances are that we know nothing else about it at

all. But do we need to? Do we want to? How many points are in it?

A certain sort of knowledge wins quizzes, and the more quizzes you do, the more of this sort of knowledge you pick up. Much of it was in your head in the first place, inculcated by indifferent teachers decades before. Some of it has found its way there by accident since. But a surprising amount of quiz knowledge comes from quizzes themselves. If you really want facts to stick, the most effective mental glue is adrenalin. Sheer competitiveness can succeed where years of education have failed.

So what facts do you need? If you really want a comprehensive guide, sad books are available which list the answers to all of the most commonly asked quiz questions. You could buy one of these, carry it everywhere and completely miss the point of the whole business. Nonetheless, there is no denying that even in the most carefully crafted quiz, certain well-worn themes tend to recur. Quizmasters are only human, and so very lazy. Unless provoked into making more of an effort by jibes and gentle punches, they will ask the same old questions time and again until they die. Here, then, is a brief resumé of the type of knowledge you will need if you too are to acquire the Gleam of Certainty. There may be no sensible reason why anyone should know what the collective noun for voles is, but that doesn't mean it won't be asked.

Science

No actual scientific or mathematical knowledge is required by most quizzes, because most participants wouldn't be able to solve a quadratic equation, let alone elucidate the fundamental principles of superstring theory. Once in a while in most quizzes, a real scientist (i.e. someone who secured a relevant A level fifteen years ago) will set the questions, and will include a few puzzlers about n-dimensional hyperspaces to show everyone that Science Can Be Fun. Everybody will complain vociferously to the landlord afterwards and the scientist will never be allowed to set the questions again. But we all agree that there should be some science included, if only to catch out those teams who know absolutely nothing about it, rather than the almost nothing that the rest of us would admit to. So, dredging our memories of schooldays (that is copying the relevant facts out of encyclopaedias) we adhere to the following pathetically limited syllabus. Right-minded educationalists would be appalled.

- $e = mc^2$. This is all anyone knows of Albert Einstein, except that he was once photographed with his tongue sticking out. Ask what the letters stand for. Don't ask what it all means. Quizzers have also heard of the Special Theory of Relativity and the General Theory of Relativity. They presume that the first one was really rather special, while the second was obviously more general. Ask anything about the unification of mass and energy, the former being a 'congealed' version of the latter, and even your closest friends may never speak to you again.

- The periodic table. This is what chemistry is to most twelve-year-olds, and to anyone taking part in a pub quiz many years later. Hydrogen (H) is number 1, helium (He) is 2 and everyone forgets that lithium (Li) is number three. The noble (or inert) gases are a familiar six-parter. Someone on your team will be convinced that they can be remembered with a mnemonic, which no one can remember. This is because the six noble gases are (in order) helium, neon, argon, krypton, xenon and radon, which together form the mnemonic HNAKXR. Joseph Priestley discovered oxygen, although no one knows why. Carbon-14 is the isotope used for carbon dating, which

might one day prove useful in establishing the age of
some of these questions.

- Boyle's Law and Charles's Law. Did you look these up
  when they were mentioned earlier? Doesn't matter if you
  did: you will still have forgotten them. The Hon. Robert
  Boyle (1627–91), old Etonian and gentleman of leisure,
  asserted that the pressure and volume of a gas are
  inversely proportional. Later Bob Charles (b. 1936), New
  Zealand golfer, connected the expansion of a gas with its
  rise in temperature. Combine the two and you get the
  Ideal Gas Law, which no one understands at all. Can't you
  just smell that musty old classroom?

Geography

The subject most of us gave up at the earliest opportunity,
exhausted by the constant effort of trying to remember what
the capital of Sierra Leone was.[1] Now, of course, there is no
effort: having got it wrong in a quiz a few weeks ago, you will
never forget the answer again. Capital cities, tallest mountains,
longest rivers, wettest seas, dryest sand, whitest snow: facts that
schoolchildren justly regard with boredom and contempt
become valuable raw material for all quizsetters. There is no
more straightforward question to ask than:

What is the state capital of Texas?

Unless it's:

Austin is the capital of which US state?

---

[1] Freetown, which was founded in 1787 by British philanthropists as a
home for former slaves. Famed for its kola nuts, pine kernels, footwear
and fish processing, Freetown also remains a cornerstone of the
international cement market.

There are fifty states, which makes a hundred questions, which can be recycled indefinitely. The twist, such as it is, is that virtually no states have their largest and best known cities as their capitals. Quiz virgins, asked the first of those two questions, will argue for days over whether it's Houston or Dallas, before someone suggests it might actually be Fort Worth. But you are rarely caught this way twice. It's certainly one way of spotting the hardened quizheads on *Fifteen-To-One*. 'What's the capital of Alabama?' asks William G Stewart. 'Montgomery,' says Hardened Quizhead, without a pause. Other contestants look on him with new respect, and vow to get him later.

- Mountains. Very high things, often with snow on top. Quiz compilers are only interested in the highest and most easily pronounceable, such as Mt McKinley (highest in USA), Kilimanjaro (highest in Africa) and Mt Logan (highest in Canada). Cerro Aconcagua, the highest mountain in South America, rarely crops up. Mount Everest, incidentally, is known in Chinese as Qomolangma, in Nepalese as Sagarmatha and in Tibetan as Mi-ti gu-ti cha-pu long-na, which can be quite an entertaining question to ask at the end of a long evening.
- Rivers. Longest is the Nile, whose 4145 miles laugh in the face of the Amazon, with its relatively feeble 4007. The Yangtze rolls in a distant third, the Mississippi (plus tributaries) is fourth, and Orinoco is the highest placed Womble in the list down at 32nd. Australia's longest river is the Murray-Darling (2330 miles), which seems only appropriate. Most questions, though, will be about European rivers, because most people just about remember that they exist. Frankfurt is on the Main, not the Rhine; otherwise the answer is usually the Volga,

the Danube or the Rhône. For 'rivers of blood' see
Politics.

Pop Music

It featured on *Mastermind* only rarely ('Your specialist questions on The Life and Works of Ozzy Osbourne start . . .
now'). *Brain of Britain* scarcely acknowledges its existence.
Fifteen-To-One prods it with the occasional bargepole, but no
more. Pub quizzes cannot do without it. Some pubs even hold
dedicated pop quizzes, in which the music-crazed landlord
plays three-second snatches of all his favourite records which
no one else recognises. It's the subject that generates the most
questions, and also the most arguments, if only because
people's knowledge of pop music varies so greatly. Most
quizzers over fifty, it is fair to say, know nothing about it, and
feel aggrieved that they should be required to answer questions on it. (The equivalent subject for those under thirty-five
is gardening.) Most younger quizzers have at least a sprinkling
of pop knowledge, usually based on the music they listened to
non-stop during their teens and early twenties. Everything
before this period is laughably ancient (Keith West's 'Excerpt
From a Teenage Opera'), while everything afterwards is just
bleeps and noise, because people forgot how to write tunes at
around the time you bought your first car.

And then there are the experts. They will be men, probably
between the ages of thirty and forty-five, and they will have a
frightening knowledge of pop music, stretching unbroken from
Hank Williams's first scratchy 78s to the latest white-label
drum 'n' bass blatherings by someone in a funny hat from
Ladbroke Grove. Not only will they know the answers to
every question that can be asked, but they will tell you the
answer before the quizmaster has finished asking it. They will
wear only black, and if they are on my team they will be
called George.

This sets almost insurmountable problems for anyone setting questions on the subject. The category 'A' quizzers, the furious oldies, will snarl at the merest mention of Sir Cliff Richard. Category 'B', the rump of mostly lapsed pop fans, will have a go at the easy ones but resent anything too obscure. Category 'C', the experts, will get everything right and wonder why the questions weren't a little more challenging. In fact George isn't that arrogant, but his penchant for clothes no lighter than very dark grey cannot help but plant suspicion in the minds of most other teams. Correctly, of course, because what he doesn't know about The Dooleys and Liquid Gold isn't worth knowing.

Questions on pop music, therefore, can only be outrageously easy or outrageously hard, according to taste. Which was Sister Sledge's only number 1 single? Who sang the first line of Band Aid's 'Do They Know It's Christmas'? Which two British politicians were mentioned by name in The Beatles' 'Taxman'?[2] If you don't know the answers, find someone wearing black who does.

Sport

Perhaps the boniest of all bones of contention, for pop music's great age divide is as nothing compared to sport's great sex divide. Oldies are going to complain anyway: their antiquity, as well as all those aches and pains in internal organs we youngsters don't know we have, is excuse enough. But sport divides humanity even more ruthlessly than pop music does. Most men, even the feeblest men, with biceps like pipe-cleaners and

---

[2] Sister Sledge's only number 1 was 'Frankie' in 1984. The infinitely better 'We Are Family' and 'Lost In Music' only reached 5 and 4 respectively. Paul Young sang the first line of 'Do They Know It's Christmas'. The politicians mentioned in 'Taxman' were Harold Wilson and Edward Heath.

knees that could knobble for England, have a knowledge of sporting matters that starts at the encyclopaedic and ends somewhere close to the psychiatric. Most women, by comparison, have just about heard of Gary Lineker. There is no way of reconciling these entirely incompatible levels of knowledge (or interest), so most male quizmasters don't bother. By pretending that women aren't there, or don't matter, you can include all manner of complicated football conundrums that will make you feel warm inside and cheer your male friends. But you will repel most women. The sexual make-up of pub quiz teams varies enormously throughout the country, but it is usually safe to say that an all-male pub quiz is the sign of a quiz in decline. Banish women, and audiences become ever smaller and more badly dressed. Sports questions should therefore be used sparingly, and as imaginatively as possible.

I say 'most women' because not all women are sports-phobes, just as not all men spend half their lives clicking up page 301 on Ceefax. The explosion in football's popularity has attracted a whole new generation of female supporters, one of whom is Tara, one of our team's occasionals at the Prince of Wales. Tara has a Spurs season ticket and a knowledge of football so extensive that the rest of us occasionally fear for her sanity – while of course deferring to her expertise at all times. Indeed Terence, who always thought he was our football expert, now goes a bit quiet whenever Tara turns up. He bears no grudge: he has merely been superseded by a greater talent. The meritocracy of quizzing allows no other response.

Football, of course, is the pre-eminent quizzing sport; the relative significance of the others is approximately proportional to the coverage they each receive in the sporting press. So don't hold your breath for many bowls questions. Nor will croquet be high on the agenda.

- Football. Essential to know all League and FA Cup winners since about 1965, plus the names of all Premiership and Football League home grounds, especially the more eccentric ones. Familiarity with the managerial career of Big Ron Atkinson is a bonus. Really there is no limit to what you might be asked about football. While no one would consider the more abstruse margins of quantum mechanics a fit subject for quiz questions, scarcely less obscure areas of football knowledge are routinely dished up. It is not inverted snobbery, or at least not wholly. It is just a belief, held as strongly as any religion, that people ought to know these things. Infuriatingly, someone on another team always does.

- Cricket. A beautiful sport in sad decline, so no one ever knows any of the answers. If you are similarly befuddled, try 'Ian Botham' or 'W G Grace', unless they want an Australian ('Donald Bradman'), West Indian ('Viv Richards') or Indian ('Sunil Gavaskar'). If a woman has set the quiz, the answer tends to be 'Imran Khan'.

- Horse racing. Derby winners, Grand National winners, top jockeys (especially those with humorous speech impediments). The five Classics crop up frequently. Which three make up the Triple Crown?[3] Which two races are for fillies only?[4] Which race might easily have been called the Bunbury?[5] Why does the horse a bloke in a pub tells you to put your shirt on always come in seventh?

---

[3] The Derby, the 2,000 Guineas, the St Leger.
[4] The other two, The Oaks and the 1,000 Guineas.
[5] The Derby. The 12th Earl of Derby and Sir Charles Bunbury set up the race, and then tossed a coin to decide whom it should be named after.

• Snooker. A mischievous one, this, for while many men
watch it on television (usually at one in the morning
when slightly the worse for wear), few of us absorb much
information about the sport. We know that Steve Davis is
'interesting', Stephen Hendry never smiles and some
Canadian with a bouffant hairstyle once scored the
maximum break of . . . er . . . what was that number
again?[6] (And what is the real maximum break, if we are
going to be pernickety about it?[7]) But many men, if
pressed, would not count snooker as a proper sport
because it is played indoors, and everyone wears bow-
ties. Many of snooker's most dedicated fans are women,
who often regard their enthusiasm as faintly shameful,
like drinking gin at breakfast. Uniquely, then, sport's
great sex divide is reversed, leading to rages and
recriminations from all-male teams who thought we were
supposed to be answering questions about sport, for
Christ's sake.

Children's Television

Whoever said 'You're only young once' obviously never went
to a pub quiz. Most quizmasters either watch too much television, or watch far too much television, and their memories
of childhood viewing habits remain especially vivid. They
have also all bought Geoff Tibballs's excellent book *The
Golden Age of Children's Television* and frequently fillet it for
questions. What was the name of the cow in *The Magic*

---

[6] 147. Cliff Thorburn was the first player to achieve the feat in the
World Championship, back in 1982.

[7] 155. After a foul stroke by your opponent, you are snookered on
all the reds, so take a colour as a free ball (1 point), the black as
colour (7 points) and then knock in all the 15 reds and colours as
usual (147 points). Easy when you know how.

Roundabout? Who was the sixth Doctor Who? Was there really a character called 'Seaman Stains' in *Captain Pugwash?*[8] Here at last is the justification for all those thousands of hours you spent glued to useless children's programmes when you were a child – programmes you had already seen many times before, because most were repeated over and over again. (A good tie-break: how many episodes of *The Herbs* were made?[9]) The cosy fog of nostalgia subverts all such memories, making us far fonder of these ramshackle old shows in retrospect than we ever were at the time. Again, this is the sort of subject that cleaves the generations. Quizzers under twenty-five have their own terrible kids' TV to remember, but unfortunately no one yet asks questions about it. Anyone over sixty just feels left out, and may mutter something about singing songs around the 'old joanna' before subsiding into a sulk. One or two people in the intervening age group will complain that they didn't have a television when they were young, or if they did, were only allowed to watch improving documentaries on BBC2. The fact that they still blame their parents for this, and not the TV-obsessed quizmaster for asking stupid questions on the subject, shows just how damaging such deprivation can be.

Soaps

Television soap operas are the sport hater's revenge. You may have a matchless grasp of Liverpool's FA Cup record, but if you can't even remember the name of the pub in Emmerdale,[10]

---

[8] Ermintrude. Colin Baker. No, it was just a foul rumour, allegedly put about by the writer and hoaxster Victor Lewis-Smith.
[9] Amazingly, only thirteen. Anyone who grew up during the 1960s or 1970s has probably seen each one of them several hundred times.
[10] The Woolpack. The bloke with the sideburns who used to run it was Amos Brearley, not Mike, as one team recently suggested.

you will never thrive in the intellectually eclectic environment of the pub quiz. Fortunately it is still the rare individual who can claim a detailed knowledge of both sport and soaps. It may be that each fulfils a similar need in people's lives (escapism tempered by bad acting). Certainly each requires a certain dedication. Both soaps and sport are in constant tumult. Any expert knowledge of either can only ever be temporary, and must be updated on a weekly if not daily basis. It's no use knowing everything about a character in *Neighbours* if he or she was kidnapped by bears six months ago, never to reappear. As in sport, the characters change constantly, even if the plots often seem a bit familiar.

The essential difference between sport and soaps, of course, is that the latter enjoy a predominantly female following. Just as most women drift into an ill-tempered doze whenever the sporting questions start, so most men knot their brows when required to display knowledge about *Coronation Street*. Quizzes only reflect the concerns of real life, and it's at such moments that you sometimes make valuable discoveries about the intricacies of your friends' domestic lives. One fellow I knew moaned incessantly whenever a soap question slipped into one of my quizzes, which it did frequently as I knew it annoyed him. It turned out that he and his wife had been waging a war of nerves over the TV remote control for years. He always wanted to watch the football. She always wanted to watch *EastEnders* or *Coronation Street*. She usually won. Mere mention of the words 'Ken Barlow' in a quiz question would drive him close to breaking point.

Sea Areas in Shipping Forecasts

A horrible subject, of no conceivable interest to anyone other than the fishing industry, Radio 4 announcers and unusually sadistic quizmasters. Which sea area literally means 'end of the

earth'?[11] Which sea area has the same name as a famous British
naval victory?[12] Most questions you will hear won't even be
that interesting.

International Vehicle Registration Letters

If you know these backwards, it may be time to stop quizzing
and find yourself a life before it's too late. When you started
going to quizzes, you cared not at all that IR is the international vehicle registration letter for Iran, and not the Republic
of Ireland (IRL) or Iraq (IRQ) as you first assumed. If someone
had asked you what Spain's letter was, you might have guessed
S, instead of shaking your head with a self-satisfied smirk and
writing down E. You now know that GBG is Guernsey, not
Gibraltar (GBZ). You have scored many points with such
knowledge, and you have no friends. (To be continued.)

Quiz 1

A book about quizzes without a few questions lying around?
It's unthinkable. Take a look at these – they are all gettable (or
at least guessable) – and contemplate them as you read the
next chapter. Don't look anything up, and above all try to
resist the temptation to flick straight to the answers now. This
may require a gargantuan effort of self-control, but I think it
might be worth it. (Some people can't help turning straight to
the last page of a thriller to see who did it: such weaklings and
retards are naturally excused.)

• Which coin made its first appearance in the 1660s, had its
  value fixed in 1717 and went out of circulation in 1816?

---

[11] Finisterre.
[12] Trafalgar.

- Which tropical disease was named after a Nigerian village where it was first reported in the 1960s?
- Hampton House in Belfast, 3 Northgate in Glasgow, India Buildings in Liverpool, Clive House in London, Olympia House in Newport and Aragon Court in Peterborough. What is the connection between these addresses?
- Which insect is so called because it was dedicated to the Virgin Mary in the Middle Ages?
- Which famous public school's school song contains this stanza?

> *The battle's to the strongest, might is always right.*
> *Trample on the weakest, glory in their plight.*
> *Let our motto be broadcast, get your blow in first.*
> *She who draws the sword last always comes off worst.*

7
Open the Box

'A successful game show host must be the sort of man who can conduct a witty conversation with a complete stranger while, at the same time, driving a car with twelve gears backwards down a mountainside.'

(Mark Goodson, game show pioneer)

In the early 1950s American television enjoyed its first (and so far only) golden age. Highbrow drama anthologies, performed live for the cameras, dominated the schedules and brought respectability to the new medium. Critics of substance, some smoking pipes, looked kindly on the efforts of a new generation of young talents who would later come to dominate Broadway, Hollywood and the wilder reaches of the American arts. For a while, as the academic Les Brown has put it, 'it seemed that the networks would be contributing a new and significant body of literature to the national culture'.[1] But then quiz shows arrived, and the golden age ended virtually overnight.

American intellectuals have never forgotten this betrayal, let alone forgiven it. Ejected so rudely from their Garden of

---

[1] 'The American Networks' by Les Brown, from *Television: A World History*, edited by Anthony Smith (Oxford University Press, 1995).

Eden, they have spent the subsequent forty years rubbishing
what they left behind, while trying to climb back in when
they thought no one was looking. They have blamed the networks, whose simple desire to maximise profits has never
wavered. They have blamed the American public for accepting lower standards with such enthusiasm. But mainly they
have blamed the quiz shows, the instrument of their banish-
ment. Over the years this modest, essentially harmless
entertainment has become a symbol of the debased society
that prefers its television cheap, undemanding and, more often
than not, presented by a middle-aged man in a shiny suit. In
Britain, which imports American cultural concerns as eagerly
as it does new varieties of breakfast cereal, the prejudice runs
even deeper. Just as some middle-class parents of the 1950s
and 1960s would not let their children watch ITV – fearful
that their minds would be warped by the sink of vileness and
degradation that was *Crossroads* – so it is still widely assumed
that no one watches quiz shows other than the elderly and the
mentally distressed. Not many of us would admit to tuning
into *Fifteen-To-One* every weekday afternoon, unless tortured
with pins. And only my quizmate George, as far as I know,
would admit to taping it every day, and catching up with the
week's episodes at the weekend. Fortunately George is
Scottish and furious, and few sensible people argue with him
about anything.

In America in the mid-1950s, the issues were rather more
clear-cut. Videotape had just been invented, which meant that
drama no longer had to be produced live. And television's
audience was expanding at a feverish rate. In 1953 only 40 per
cent of American homes had a set. Within two years that
figure almost doubled. The first Americans to buy television
sets had been middle class, with middle-class incomes and
middle-class tastes. Now the working classes were joining in.
Ratings were beginning to matter. Sponsorship was on the up.

A genuine mass medium was coming into existence. Live productions of serious plays were not what these new viewers wanted to watch. They wanted quiz shows and thousands of identical western series. The forces of historical inevitability could not be argued with. Or, to put it another way, the golden age of American television was only ever going to last until people started watching it.

The first of the big money quiz shows was launched on the CBS network on 7 June 1955. *The $64,000 Question* was based on an old radio show, *Take It or Leave It*, in which contestants were asked questions of increasing difficulty, doubling their winnings with each correct answer. CBS took this simple template and added greed. On *Take It or Leave It* the jackpot had been $64; on *The $64,000 Question* you won that much for answering just one question. Winnings then climbed in a pleasant geometric curve up to $512, after which they were rounded down to the nearest thousand for ease of salivation. At any time contestants could call a halt to the proceedings and take what they had won. Not that many did. Even if you lost, there were consolation prizes. Once past $8,000, every loser picked up a brand-new Cadillac. To win the full $64,000 you had to answer just eleven questions correctly, although this process tended to take several weeks. The final questions, if you made it that far, were obscure to the point of lunacy. A US Marine, Richard S McCutchen, became the first person to land the jackpot when he named all the dishes served at a dinner hosted by King George VI in 1939 in honour of the French President, Albert Lebrun.[2] Until that point no one had realised that the Marines provided such a thorough training.

---

[2] Consommé, quenelles, filet de truite saumonée, petit pois à la françaises, sauce maltaise, and corbeille, accompanied by Chateau d'Yquem and Madeira Sercial. Yum yum.

The $64,000 Question was an instant and massive success.
Each Sunday night 84 per cent of all American television sets
were tuned to the show. Restaurant and cinema owners would
shut up shop for the evening, so that they could go home to
watch. The sponsor's product, Revlon snow peach lipstick,
sold out everywhere – the only known occasion quizzing has
ever impinged on the world of high fashion.
Contestants queued up to demonstrate mastery of their
chosen subjects. Ordinary Joes found it easier to get on the
show than academic types: the show's producers felt that they
would be more popular with viewers. Even a handful of
celebrities were persuaded to take part. Jack Benny got one
question right, winning $64, and declined to progress any fur-
ther. Randolph Churchill, answering questions on English
History, came unstuck on question 2, when he could not
remember the derivation of the term 'boycott'.[3]
    In retrospect, it seems remarkable that anyone believed any
of this for a moment. The top prize was, for its time, a stag-
gering amount of money, worth well over five times the
amount in today's flabbier currency. American television was
not exactly rigorously regulated, and before long the competition between big money quiz shows became intense. In the
wake of *The $64,000 Question* came *High Finance, Can Do, Twenty
One, Dotto, The Big Surprise, Giant Step* and perhaps the most
imaginatively titled of them all, *The $64,000 Challenge*.
    Not all of these were entirely honest. The shows' producers

---

[3] In 1880 the Irish Land League refused to have any dealings with
Captain C C Boycott (1832–97), a land agent in County Mayo, as a
means of coercing him to reduce rents. This is now a regular pub
quiz question, frequently accompanied by chucklesome comments
regarding G Boycott (b. 1940), the Yorkshire and England opening
batsman whose behaviour and attitudes have occasionally elicited a
similar response.

would probably have said, in mitigation, that they were in the entertainment business. Their job, as they saw it, was to provide a spectacle to entrance the shows' huge and adoring audiences. In fact it had probably never occurred to them that honesty was an especially high priority. If their business were not so competitive, they would never have offered such inflated prizes. It was only sensible to ensure that the more charismatic contestants thrived, while the dorks were shown the door. The only snag with this policy was that someone would eventually find out about it.

The first accusations surfaced in 1957. A contestant on *Dotto* claimed that his opponent had been given a notebook full of the correct answers. Then Herbert Stempel, a contestant on *Twenty One*, revealed that he had been instructed to lose by the show's producers because they wanted his dashing WASP opponent Charles van Doren to win. The producers sued poor Stempel for libel, but as more such tales emerged, the New York City District Attorney convened a grand jury to investigate the whole issue of quiz fixing. Producers and sponsors cheerfully defended their actions, but the evidence against them was now overwhelming. Stempel was vindicated, van Doren ruined, and Robert Redford's 1994 film of the case, *Quiz Show*, was nominated for four Oscars, including Best Picture.

Big money television quiz shows vanished almost as suddenly as they had arrived. Hal March, the show's oleaginous host, asked the last $64,000 Question on 2 November 1958. The audience had lost faith, and sponsors were scuttling for cover. Quizzes would return to American TV in time, but their prime time days were over. Meanwhile Ralph Fiennes went on to *The English Patient*, and global megastardom.

A British version of *The $64,000 Question*, ingeniously retitled *The 64,000 Question* because they weren't allowed to give away

64,000 of anything, let alone dollars, ran for a couple of years in the late 1950s. But other shows, based on the same template, survived rather longer. The American heyday of the quiz show had coincided, not inconveniently, with the launch of ITV, the country's first commercial channel. The BBC, after a near twenty-year monopoly, had settled into an easy schedule of improving talks, live opera and classic theatre, interspersed with the occasional programme people actually wanted to see. Peter Black, the distinguished TV critic, later wrote: 'Until ITV arrived the public . . . had never seen Sunday night variety, or an American drama series; most important, they had never seen anyone earn a pound note for correctly distinguishing his left foot from his right, or a wife win a refrigerator for whitewashing her husband in thirty seconds from NOW.'[4] Obviously such a disgraceful state of affairs had to be corrected. In its first four days ITV introduced four game shows; by May 1957 there were eight a week. In among these were two out-and-out quiz shows, both based on the American model, and both destined to outlive their forebears by more than a decade.

Double Your Money and *Take Your Pick* made their debuts in ITV's first week, having both enjoyed previous incarnations on Radio Luxembourg. *Double Your Money* was hosted by Hughie Green, a former child prodigy and film actor whose glistening brand of Canadian insincerity would infest TV light entertainment for twenty-five years. *The $64,000 Question*'s format – sympathetic everyman contestants answering questions of rapidly increasing difficulty and doubling their winnings each time – was accurately reproduced, with one vital difference. American contestants had won $64 for their first correct answer; Hughie's downtrodden pensioners picked up just a single pound note. Top prize under ITV rules was £1,000, and

---

[4] *The Mirror in the Corner* (Hutchinson, 1972).

remained so for years. (Even in the mid-1980s no one could win more than £2,000.) The intention was to prevent the corruption that had brought down the American shows. The effect was to breed a culture of quiz show meanness that has never been fully eradicated. On *Double Your Money* prizewinners really earned their bounty. Hughie patronised them relentlessly, and indeed us, who he usually called 'all these good people at home'. As winnings climbed to a respectable level, so contestants were locked in the inevitable soundproof glass booth with headphones. Hughie asked his questions, while an enormous clock counted off the seconds behind. Even small children knew that Hughie didn't want his contestants to win, for all his fulsome encouragements. But the format was as airtight as the booth. *Double Your Money* did not vacate the Top 20 ratings chart for thirteen years.

Yin to Hughie's Yang, or possibly id to his superego, was Michael Miles, the tall, balding, eagle-nosed and oddly threatening host of *Take Your Pick*. Hughie wanted his audience to love him. Miles couldn't care less. Players had to answer three questions correctly to be given a key to a numbered box, in which they would find a voucher for a prize. 'Open the box or take the money' was the dilemma. If contestants were keen to open the box, Miles would offer them more and more money, which he would fan out in his hand so that it looked as though it was worth having. This was quiz show as blood sport. Contestants taking the money were deemed to be party poopers, while anyone who opened the box and found only a booby prize became the object of an unspoken ridicule which Miles gleefully failed to conceal behind his show of sympathy. Peter Black talked of his 'slightly mutinous and defiant air, suggesting a public school man gone wrong'.[5] When *Take Your Pick* was

---

[5] Ibid.

resuscitated by Carlton in 1992, the host chosen was Des O' Connor, a man far too amiable for the role. The original show matched *Double Your Money* for longevity and popularity; the updated version struggles on as an occasional summer filler.

Double Your Money and *Take Your Pick* took the American format and transformed it into something ineradicably British. This is a reversal of the natural order of things. Britain usually invents; other smarmier nations then develop and exploit. The quiz show, by contrast, was wholly American in origin. Brits adapted the genre to suit local conditions, but did it so well that no one knew the difference. It's hard to imagine a TV programme more quintessentially British than *University Challenge* – to the extent that, unconsciously, I have just found myself describing it as a 'programme' rather than a 'show'. Yet Bamber Gascoigne's pension started life in the 1950s as an American game show called *College Bowl*. Only thirty episodes were ever made. The 'quintessentially British' version ran for twenty-six years.

All assessments of this golden quarter-century must begin and end with Bamber. Few light entertainment figures of our time have become universally known by just a single name, and a good proportion of those (Madonna, Sting) only have one name anyway. Otherwise we are left only with the holy trinity of Cilla, Elvis and that god of football in distant foreign parts, Bobbycharlton. And yet Bamber is not far behind. Thanks to a grave shortage of alternative Bambers, he has remained the only famous Bamber of our time, and probably the only non-famous Bamber too. Fashions in children's names change all the time, but they have never changed quickly enough to admit 'Bamber' into the fold. The only threat to his supremacy came from an entirely unexpected direction, when for a few years he was only the second most famous Gascoigne in the country. But as a Bamber he has been unique, as has been his remarkable programme.

For in those heady, fluid years, *University Challenge* managed to achieve and maintain its popularity without, it seems, any compromise with popular culture at all. Intellectually it was on a par with Radio 4's more abstruse quizzes. Bamber never called anyone Mr Stemp or Mr Wasilewski, but you felt he would have if he could have. His questions were often fantastically tough. Most graduates who watched the programme realised how little they remembered of their own degree subject, let alone everybody else's. The young shavers on the programme, though, knew everything, buzzing in with the answer before Bamber was even halfway through his list of Assyrian kings. When my own college conducted auditions in the late 1970s, the proceedings were soon hijacked by odd-looking postgraduate chemists no one had ever met before, and whose range of knowledge left the rest of us feeling like lower primates. They were knocked out in the first round.

In 1987, after several years of being shunted around the ITV schedules – Sunday morning after *Morning Service* was latterly the height of its ambition – *University Challenge* was put to rest. Bamber receded into private life, and most of us assumed that was that. Not so. Granada had kept faith with the format, and in 1995 found an alternative buyer in BBC2. The programme was restored, theme tune and all, with Jeremy Paxman in the chair. Purists, a handful of whom were still alive, objected to the change in questionmaster. Bamber, though, was delighted to give way. He felt twenty-six years had been enough. As it is, *University Challenge* under Paxman has become more popular than ever. Kindly scheduled by a succession of BBC2 controllers, it has become one of those programmes that defines its audience. Middle class, competitive, faintly over-educated, and with nothing better to do on a Wednesday evening, *University Challenge* viewers identify themselves as closely with their favourite programme as *Coronation Street* fans do with theirs. I have a friend who is rich, successful, far too busy and almost impossible to get hold of. The only time you can be sure of finding him at home is just after *University Challenge* has finished.

Newspaper editors, trained to use words like 'Zeitgeist' without laughing, have picked up on this unlikely fervour. If a contestant did something daft on, say, *Family Fortunes*, the press would take little notice. (Only the man who froze during the Big Money challenge and answered every question with the word 'turkey' has achieved any level of notoriety.) But when, in December 1996, Birkbeck College in London recorded the most crushing defeat in *University Challenge*'s long history, losing 360–40 to Manchester, the news made several front pages. 'Starter For Ten: Who Put the Birk in Birkbeck?' asked the *Daily Mail*. 'Universthicky Challenge: Bunch of Birkbecks TV Flop,' mocked the *Daily Mirror*. Even *The Times* ('Quiz Team Universally Challenged') had a go. Birkbeck's students were reported to be 'demoralised' by the result. In *The Times Higher Educational Supplement*, a lachrymose correspondent revealed that 'staff at the college are predicting that recruitment will be down by 10 per cent next year'. Six months later, a journalist in the same paper came to a stark conclusion. 'Whether rightly or wrongly, the programme plays a key role in shaping the public's perception of a university, and in defining the state of British higher education.'[6] Rightly or wrongly: that's the bit I like. (He meant wrongly, of course.) When Birkbeck reached the final in the following series, losing bravely to an omniscient quartet from Magdalen College, Oxford, they were commonly held to have restored the college's reputation. Meanwhile the captain of the Magdalen team, who was young, female and pretty, was instantly launched on a lucrative media career. The show's impact is

---

[6] Phil Baty, *The Times Higher Educational Supplement*, 13 June 1997.

undeniable. No out-and-out quiz show has survived so long, and remained so fresh.

No one remembers what prize you get for winning *University Challenge*, although having your hand shaken by someone famous is known to figure somewhere. It's amazing, in our materialistic society, how little this seems to matter. But the poverty of the prizes offered by *Double Your Money* and *Take Your Pick* set a precedent for British game shows that has rarely been challenged. Anglia's *Sale of the Century* (1972–83) started with £1 questions and then moved up, via trickier £3 questions, to the ultimate challenge of £5 questions at the show's climax. Several contestants visibly buckled under the strain. (Peter Fenn, the show's magnificently cheesy organist, cropped up in 1997 as a contestant on *Fifteen-To-One*. His job title was 'retired musician'. He was knocked out in the first round.) *Going For Gold* (1987–96) invited contestants from all over Europe to compete for the chance of winning a holiday abroad which, if they were lucky, was not the country they came from in the first place. As the quiz was conducted in English by Henry Kelly, who will never use one word when the entire contents of the *Concise Oxford* will do, most foreign participants were professional translators with several degrees, and even they were usually beaten by truck drivers from Hull. But the difficulty of finding appropriate contestants was offset by the programme's environmentally friendly use of them. If you lost one day, you just came back the following day in a different coloured jacket and tried again. Virtually everyone made it through to the heats of the quarter-finals, or the quarter-finals of the heats, or possibly both. Each series went on for ever. Anyone who was unemployed, housebound or otherwise compelled to watch television every weekday at 1:50 p.m. during the years of *Going For Gold* knows the true meaning of despair.

Contestant research has always been an inexact science. Some shows seek out the well-informed and the learned, while others are so determined to give 'ordinary people' a go that they sometimes find contestants with no apparent general knowledge at all. Jim Bowen's darts quiz *Bullseye* (1981–93) was notorious for the dimness of its contestants. Many of them couldn't even throw darts. In Yorkshire TV's *3-2-1* (1978–87) – based on a Spanish original, and it might still have been in Spanish for all that anyone understood it – one round I vividly remember was on 20th-century world leaders. Ted Rogers, whose hair had grown more unfeasibly purple with each series, gave the first name of a famous individual. The contestant had to give the surname. Not hard, unless you were a contestant on *3-2-1*. First question to first contestant was 'Winston'. First contestant thought a bit, said 'Churchill', and the studio audience broke into spontaneous applause. Next question, to next contestant: 'Adolf'. Answer: 'Hitler'. Whooping and whistling. Contestants obviously getting the gist. Third question, to third contestant: 'Margaret'. (This was the mid-1980s, and you sensed that Ted yielded to no one in his adoration of the Leaderene.) Big smile from third contestant, who said 'Thatcher'. Screams of delight from audience; paramedics on standby. Finally, contestant four, and question four. 'Dag,' said Ted. Contestant four looked mystified. 'Dag,' said Ted again, as millions of viewers bawled 'Hammarskjöld!' at the screen. Contestant four obviously hadn't a clue, but may have watched the snooker on TV the previous night. 'Mountjoy?' he asked hopefully.

The best quiz shows combine this sadistic edge with a prize-free puritanism that has outlived all those strict regulations preventing huge cash handouts. In the mid-1990s you could pocket anything up to £20,000 on the brasher ITV game shows, but until 1997 the most prestigious prize of all was the repellent glass bowl handed annually to winners of

Mastermind, and probably dropped and smashed on the way home on the bus. To have been champion of *Mastermind* carries a unique cachet in quizzing circles. Kevin Ashman has won everything else, sometimes twice, but it is for his 1995 *Mastermind* win – and his record combined score of 41 – that his fame (such as it is) rests. He and the rest of the *Mastermind* club meet on the third Wednesday of every month in a West End wine bar. 'Not big drinkers,' says the wine bar's owner. 'Unlike the Mensa lot. Now they're a real bunch of nutters.'

Mastermind, in keeping with its mythical status, has generated some memorable folklore. Everybody knows that its creator Bill Wright, who died in 1981, had been a POW in the last war and wanted to recreate the atmosphere of a wartime interrogation. The spotlight and the leather chair were designed to make contestants feel that they were being grilled under the fiercest pressure. The title music he chose was called 'Approaching Menace'. The same chair was used throughout the programme's twenty-six seasons, transported around the country by lorry. Magnus Magnusson always refused to sit in it. In 1979 students at the University of Coleraine kidnapped the chair and demanded a £50 ransom for their Cambodia Relief Fund. After tense negotiations they gave it back. No money changed hands.

At its peak in the late 1970s *Mastermind* attracted a regular audience of 12 million, and has been widely credited with fuelling the quiz boom. '*Mastermind* has spawned a national obsession with general knowledge, from popular board games to raucous pub quizzes,' said a *Times* leader on the day after its cancellation. I'm not so sure. (Raucous? Pub quizzes?) It was the element of confrontation, as much as the questions, that pulled in such healthy audiences. Most of us only ever knew the answers to a fraction of the questions. But *Mastermind* certainly rode the quiz wave, and was still making headlines in its final year, when one contestant chose as her specialist subject the history and treatment of anorexia (she had been a sufferer), and another opted for punk rock. Some of us had been waiting a long time to hear Magnus use the words 'Sid Vicious' in a *Mastermind* question. He did not let us down. In fact, only a handful of specialist subjects were ever rejected as too obscure. 'Orthopaedic Bone Cement in Total Hip Replacement' failed to impress the selectors, as did, astonishingly, 'The Banana Industry' and 'Routes to Anywhere in Mainland Britain From Letchworth by Road'. Who said quizzers had no lives?

Which brings us neatly back to *Fifteen-To-One*, the daily teatime quiz show on Channel 4. *University Challenge* draws the middle classes, *Mastermind* pulls in the sadists and Nazi war criminals, but *Fifteen-To-One* is the quiz show for the connoisseur. William G Stewart, a former redcoat who used to produce *Bless This House*, walks out on to his electric-blue set every afternoon armed with a sheaf of questions, and proceeds to eliminate twelve of the fifteen contestants before the commercial break. It is a wonderfully cruel game. You get no credit for a right answer, but you lose one of your three lives for every wrong answer. If you get an answer right, you nominate the next person to be asked a question. The last three contestants left qualify for the day's final in part two. Each of them has three new lives, and each correct answer is worth ten points. So the game continues, with each contestant losing a life for every wrong answer, and choosing whether to take another question or nominate one of the others after every right answer. The last player left is the winner, who then tries to score as many points as possible to secure a place on the Finals Board. After sixty-four daily shows, the top fifteen on the Finals Board graduate to the Grand Final, the winner of which receives an Etruscan pot from William G's younger and prettier wife Laura. All episode winners are invited to take part again in the following series. It sounds complicated, but if you watch it every day for several years, you soon get the hang.

The great mystery of *Fifteen-To-One* is why any contestant agrees to go on it at all. The chances of winning a prize are virtually nil. The chances of looking a fool, by contrast, are high. If you fail to answer your first two questions, you are out and that's it. The light goes out, you sit down and someone else gets the easy question about King Lear's three daughters. It can happen to anyone. All you can say is that you were unlucky. My friend Bill was unlucky, and his friends replay the videotape of his humiliation at parties to this day.

But sooner or later everyone fails. There have been serial winners who know everything, who reached the Grand Final several times but never did well enough to win the contest outright. Then one day their luck runs out. (Often it's a question about the Scottish legal system, of which no one knows anything.) They are eliminated, with nothing to show for their efforts besides a few memories and a nagging sense of under-achievement. (Not surprisingly, the show is very popular with the elderly.) Many *Fifteen-To-One* fans remember Simon Holmes, an actor from Tufnell Park in north London, and in earlier years a fantastically lugubrious nurse called Chris Russon. They were the great survivors, who returned in series after series, unflappable under pressure, and apt to nod imperceptibly just as they worked out the answer. Neither ever topped the Finals Board (the only other way to win a prize) or won a Grand Final, although both came second. In the end they failed like everyone else: it just took them longer to do so.

Both *Mastermind* (in its latter years) and *University Challenge* (since its rebirth) have been accused of 'dumbing down': making the questions easier to compensate for thicker contestants. It may well seem that way, especially to viewers who have watched a lot of TV quizzes over the years and now know many more answers than they used to. In fact there is no evidence that either programme has ever relaxed its standards. *Mastermind* remained rigorous to the last, while *University Challenge*'s much criticised rounds on popular culture regularly bemuse students who have been chosen for their in-depth knowledge of Gothic architecture. Meanwhile *Fifteen-To-One*, watched by none of the people who make such airy accusations, has actually 'dumbed up'. Its questions are appreciably harder than they were, partly because most of the easy ones were used up many series ago, but mainly because contestants know more and are less easily caught out. By the time a three-month run of *Fifteen-To-One* reaches its Grand Final, the standard has become fearsome. On *University Challenge* you have time to think and you have team-mates to help you. On *Mastermind* you were on your own, but you had the luxury of being able to get a few questions wrong. On *Fifteen-To-One* you have to get virtually every question right, and you have about two and a half seconds in which to do it. The pressure is intense. Fortunately these men and women know their onions, and just about everything else as well.

It does help, however, if you watch the show regularly. *Fifteen-To-One* questions have a tendency to appear again and again, although with 190 half-hour shows a year to feed, you can hardly blame their question-setters for a little judicious recycling. But their questions are invariably well composed, and having been properly researched, have the enormous advantage of being right. Compilers of pub quizzes happily admit to copying questions from *Fifteen-To-One*. Why steal from any but the best?

Chris and George refuse point-blank to audition for *Fifteen-To-One*. They have their pride, and they know too many people with VCRs. Terence went to an audition, got a couple wrong and was rejected, to his and everyone else's disappointment. And me? Well, that's another story.

*

In September 1998 ITV launched a new prime-time quiz show, *Who Wants to Be a Millionaire?* Hosted by Chris Tarrant, who couldn't have been earning much less, it offered the ultimate game show prize – a cool million, neatly parcelled into wads of £50 notes. 'Where did they get the money?' we all wondered as we rang the premium phone lines (77p per call) in desperate attempts to get on the show. All you had to do was answer a multiple choice question (easy), leave your details after the beep and wait to be rung back after 'the computer' (man with clipboard) had selected you at random from many thousands of equally worthy callers. I rang dozens of times under a whole football team of credible aliases, but the bastards never once called me back.

Ten callers were chosen for each show, and then whisked in long cars to the studio, where they had to answer another multiple choice question (even easier than before). The fastest to press the right button on the keypad (2.06 seconds usually did the trick) was hauled up by Chris and invited to play for the million. What could be simpler?

The tricky bit, though, was winning it. The first five questions, which took the prize up to £1,000, were often comically easy, presumably to ensure that everyone won something. The next five, which took it up to £32,000, were less straightforward but usually negotiable. (One lucky woman had this for £16,000: 'Complete the title of this famous portrait: "The Laughing . . ."' Her four choices were hyena, peasant, fool and cavalier. She only just avoided laughing herself.)

And the last five questions were fantastically hard. *Mastermind* champions might have been in with a chance, but all of them had been expertly weeded out by 'the computer', which showed an uncanny preference for contestants who were not likely to win very much. The most anyone managed to take home in that first series was £64,000.

Odd, that. Forty years ago $64,000 had been the ultimate

goal, drooled over by millions. Now £64,000 was a mere consolation prize. But the millions were still tuning in, and ringing
the premium phone lines, and shouting at the screen when
someone didn't know that the capital of California was
Sacramento. *Who Wants to Be a Millionaire?* ran over ten consecutive evenings, and made for gripping television, just as *The
$64,000 Question* must have done all those years ago. Who
wants to be a millionaire? I do. Don't you?

Answers to Quiz 1

The coin that made its first appearance in the 1660s, had its
value fixed in 1717 and went out of circulation in 1816 was the
guinea. The tropical disease named after a Nigerian village
where it was first reported in the 1960s was Lassa fever.
Hampton House in Belfast, 3 Northgate in Glasgow, India
Buildings in Liverpool, Clive House in London, Olympia
House in Newport and Aragon Court in Peterborough are all
passport offices. The insect dedicated to the Virgin Mary
during the Middle Ages was the ladybird. And that notable
stanza came from the school song of St Trinian's.

Quiz 2

- Human adults each have 206 bones. Are human babies
  born with the same number of bones, more bones, or
  fewer bones?
- In 1903 Earl Russell queued all night to get the first ever
  what?
- Which European nation was the first to give women the
  vote and has also come last most often in the Eurovision
  Song Contest?

- The name of the writer of *Birds of the West Indies*, which was first published in 1936, became famous after it was borrowed for the name of a fictional character in a series of novels. What was the name of the obscure ornithologist?
- Derek Jarman's film *Sebastiane* has the distinction of being the only British film ever to be released in Britain with subtitles in English. In what language was the dialogue?

8

The Knowledge, Part II

*'If I ever felt inclined to be timid as I was going into a
room full of people, I would say to myself, "You're the
cleverest member of one of the cleverest families in the
cleverest class of the cleverest nation in the world. Why
should you be frightened?"'*

(Beatrice Webb)

The Classics

A potent source of quiz questions, and also of drunken arguments over whether such questions should be asked any more.
Since Latin and Greek were abandoned by the state education
system, an entire dimension of knowledge and understanding
has effectively vanished, accompanied by the answers to many
good questions. If a man had a sororate marriage, who would
he have taken for his wife?[1] Commonly used in mathematics,
how is the Latin phrase meaning 'which was to be shown or
proved' usually abbreviated?[2] That last one I stole from *Fifteen-
To-One*: the man who failed to answer it just shook his head
furiously, appalled that anyone should be expected to know
such a thing. But people did know such things twenty or
thirty years ago, and anyone who has done time in the British

---

[1] His wife's sister.
[2] Q.E.D.

public school system knows them still. A handful of state schools are rumoured to teach the classics, in much the same way that Lord Lucan is rumoured to be alive and well and living in Oswestry. Overall, though, this is a playing field rather less level than you would expect to find in the grounds of Eton or Harrow. In quizzing terms the decline of Latin and Greek has opened up one of the widest cultural gaps of them all. Devious quizmasters can exploit it with ridiculous ease.

More democratic, strangely enough, is classical mythology, which even quite young people have managed to absorb from picture books with very large print. Actually this is unfair, as I recently got a question right because of my in-depth knowledge of the film *Clash of the Titans*, starring Harry Hamlin as Perseus and Laurence Olivier as Zeus. Academic knowledge may fail you, but useless old movies will never let you down. Do not forget that all the planets are named after Roman gods, and that only the Greek goddess of victory has a running shoe named after her.[3] Ares is the Greek god of war; Aries is the ram with the golden fleece (21 March–19 April). If you come up against an unfamiliar god or goddess, do not be disheartened. If it sounds laid back and feline (Ra, Isis, Min, Khepri), it's probably Egyptian. If it sounds cold and bearded (Thor, Odin, Frigg, Balder), it's probably Norse. Egypt's most amusing god, incidentally, was Amun, the god of Thebes, who was usually represented as a man with an erect penis. Sadly this fact rarely appears in pub quizzes.

Politics

Any alien civilisation that tuned into our radio stations, watched our TV or had our broadsheet newspapers delivered

---

[3] Nike. Not Adidas (named after the company's founder, Adolf Dassler) or Puma (big grey cat which runs very fast).

to its door every day would surely conclude that we are a nation in thrall to political discourse. They would imagine us discussing the finer points of the day's parliamentary debates over a few drinks in the pub each evening, before racing home to watch *Question Time*, having put *Panorama* on the timer. Only when they landed their spacecraft in the paved square behind the Prince of Wales, and sidled in to sample the galactically notorious Tuesday night quiz, would they begin to understand how wrong they had been.

The pub quiz provides definitive proof that the British don't care a tuppenny hoop for politics. Questions are asked, frequently in fact, but few of them require knowledge of or interest in the subject. For instance: who is the only British Prime Minister ever to have played first-class cricket?[4] Which British MP disappeared from Miami Beach in 1973, claiming to be Joseph Markham?[5] Who is the only American President ever to have been divorced?[6] Whereas if you asked for the name of the current Leader of the House or the Shadow Agriculture Secretary, a great wave of boredom would engulf the pub's clientele, and possibly your entire quiz. Later on, someone would draw you into a corner and tell you to get a grip.

Maybe it is the media's obsession with politics and politicians, or the constant fevered activity, or the endless procession of talking heads in suits assessing the fevered activity of other talking heads in suits, or just the fact that nothing ever changes at all, except to get worse. Pub quizzes,

---

[4] Sir Alec Douglas-Home, who played ten matches between 1924 and 1927 for six different teams. Wisden's obituary described him as 'useful'.
[5] John Stonehouse. Extra point if you remembered that his secretary-cum-mistress (and subsequently wife) was Sheila Buckley.
[6] Ronald Reagan.

however, must keep their audience entertained, which is why that any question referring to the Westland Affair of 1986 will ask which was the other helicopter company involved,[7] and which two Cabinet Ministers resigned as a consequence,[8] and *nothing else at all*, because no one knows, remembers or cares.

British History

Much the most useful reference book on this subject is *1066 and All That*, by W C Sellar and R J Yeatman (1930). In its admirable intention of taking the piss out of history teaching through the ages ('History is not what you thought. *It is what you can remember.* All other history defeats itself.'), this small volume accurately reproduces pub quizzing's own strikingly narrow history syllabus. Sellar and Yeatman insist that there are only two dates you ever need to remember – 55 BC and 1066 – and even for serious quizzers there are probably no more than half a dozen others:

- 1154 (Thomas à Becket killed).
- 1215 (Magna Carta).
- 1485 (not sure about this one, but it's something important, I feel it in my bones).
- 1649 (Charles I beheaded, as memorably played by Alec Guinness in the film *Cromwell*).
- 1901 (Queen Victoria finally dies. Timothy West takes over).
- 1936 (Abdication crisis. Edward Fox abdicates).
- 1966 (England win World Cup).

---

[7] Sikorsky.
[8] Michael Heseltine in a giant hair-tossing tantrum and later, more circumspectly, Leon Brittan.

These days the teaching of history in schools concentrates increasingly on the way ordinary people used to live in days gone by, and how awful the toilets were. For most quizzers, though, history still means kings, queens, battles and death. Who was the last king of England to die in battle?[9] In which country was George III buried?[10] For generations history teachers relied on the sheer oddity of most British kings and queens to keep their pupils amused; decades later the oddities are all we remember. Which English queen owned 150 wigs?[11] Which English queen never visited England?[12] Again, films and television inform much of a quizzer's historical knowledge. George III was of course Nigel Hawthorne, and his son the Prince Regent was Hugh Laurie out of *Blackadder*. Laurence Olivier or Kenneth Branagh was Henry V (delete to taste). Glenda Jackson was Elizabeth I; Keith Michell was Henry VIII. Anthony Hopkins played someone or other, but right now none of us can remember who.

Literature

A potentially troublesome area, for despite all the Penguin Classics ostentatiously brandished on public transport, few people actually read any. Nineteenth-century novels tend to be too long, 20th-century novels too obscure, and a few stinkers, like *Finnegan's Wake*, pull off the Spring Double. Even

---

[9] Richard III at Bosworth Field. This was what 1485 was all about. Like Louis XIV and Napoleon Bonaparte, Richard III was born with teeth.

[10] Hanover. Accept Germany if violence is threatened.

[11] Elizabeth I. She also stuffed cloth in her mouth to make up for her lack of teeth.

[12] Richard I's wife Queen Berengaria. He himself spent only six months of his ten-year reign in the country, as he had pressing Crusades to attend to elsewhere.

the supposedly educated middle classes settle down on the beach these days with a cheesy American thriller, and few of them bother to hide it within a hollowed-out hardback of *The Brothers Karamazov*. As it is, current wisdom has it that only women read books nowadays, and this is regularly borne out on *Fifteen-To-One* by the horrified reactions of men asked to name anyone who ever wrote anything. '*The Bostonians, The Europeans, Portrait of a Lady,*' says William G Stewart. 'Novels by which 19th- and 20th-century American-born author?' 'Frederick Forsyth?' says Sorry Male. As the buzzer sounds, he instantly realises he should have said Robert Ludlum instead.

Once again we must rely on film and television for the core of our knowledge. Only when a book has been made into an all-star feature film, preferably shot in Venice, does it acquire any genuine cultural resonance. People buy the tie-in paperback as a memento and place it happily on their shelves, relieved that they will never be forced to read it. *Howard's End* and *A Passage to India* are well-known novels by E M Forster, and even better known films by Merchant/Ivory and David Lean. *The Longest Journey* is the only one of Forster's novels never to have been filmed, and so is almost unknown. This could be the basis of an interesting question, if only anyone knew the answer to it.

In pub quizzes, then, literature is often marginalised, if not completely disregarded. Any depth of knowledge you enjoy of the subject will be wasted. Instead such questions as there are will devolve into three not-terribly-broad categories, Poetry, Dickens and Shakespeare. Occasionally someone will put in a question about last year's Booker Prize, but only if they are feeling mean.

• Poetry. Obviously no one reads modern poetry, other than professional poets, professional poets' families and the poetry reviewer of the *Sunday Times*. If Simon Armitage is

the most famous contemporary poet, it is because he is
often on Radio 4, and because we have all read
somewhere that he is the most famous contemporary poet.
Any question about his poetry would assume too much.

Most poets, if they are lucky, are remembered for a few
over-familiar lines, all of which you will be asked to
identify sooner or later. 'If I should die, think only this of
me:/That there's some corner of a foreign field/That is
for ever England.' Yes, that's Rupert Brooke's life and
career summed up, or at least it would be if he had not
also written: 'Stands the Church clock at ten to
three?/And is there honey still for tea?' Philip Larkin
wrote, 'They fuck you up, your mum and dad.'
Wordsworth wandered lonely as a cloud that floats on
high o'er vales and hills. (The Latin name for daffodils,
incidentally, is *Narcissus pseudonarcissus*.) As for Gray's
'Elegy in a Country Churchyard', the answer to the usual
question is 'Stoke Poges'. Alfred, Lord Tennyson held the
post of Poet Laureate for forty-two years. John Betjeman
wished he'd had more sex. That's about it for poetry.

• Charles Dickens. Again, no need to have read a single one
of his books: seeing the film or remembering the fact from
a previous quiz will always suffice. Sydney Carton died on
the scaffold in *A Tale of Two Cities* ('It was the best of
times, it was the worst of times, . . .'). Wackford Squeers
taught at Dotheboys Hall in *Nicholas Nickleby*. And Albert
Finney took the title role in the musical version of *Scrooge*.
Dickens always faced north when writing. His third
Christian name was Huffham.

• Shakespeare. Fantastically fertile ground for dedicated
quizzers, who think they know more about the plays than
the misguided fools who pay to see them. What is the
connection between Ganymede in *As You Like It*, Cesario
in *Twelfth Night* and Balthazar the lawyer in *The Merchant*

of Venice?[13] Who actually was the Merchant of Venice?[14]
What gift was sent as an insult to Henry V by the
Dauphin of France to remind him of his youthful follies?[15]
Shakespeare questions dignify the meanest quiz. They
look highbrow. They sound, smell and taste highbrow.
And most are quite easy, so we all feel hugely smug when
we get them right. Hamlet, incidentally, is by far the
largest part in the canon, with 1569 lines. Iago (1117) has
more lines than Othello (888). Shakespeare spelt his
surname in eleven different ways.

The Seven Wonders of the Ancient World

As familiar to quizzers as cheese and onion crisps, and as
likely to stick in your throat. Lazy question setters, who need
to find a seven-pointer from somewhere but can't be bothered
to think too hard, will always head straight for the Seven
Wonders, confident that most teams will think of four straight
away, and then bang their heads against the wall, spill drinks
and kick each other under the table trying to remember the
other three. The full list is as follows:

- The Colossus of Rhodes, which was completed by Chares
  in about 280 BC, and destroyed by an earthquake fifty
  years later. Legend has it that the bronze statue was built
  astride the entrance to the harbour and that ships could
  pass between his legs. Of the Seven Wonders, this is the
  one most female quizzers tend to remember.
- The Hanging Gardens of Babylon. Built in 40 BC by King
  Nebuchadnezzar, who may not have guessed that, 2,000

---

[13] All women dressed as men.
[14] Antonio. Not Shylock. Sorts sheep from goats etc.
[15] Tennis balls.

years later, his name would most frequently be used to denote a large and expensive bottle of wine.

- The Pyramids of Egypt. The Great Pyramid of Cheops, standing 481 feet high, was the tallest structure in the world for more than 4,000 years, until overtaken in 1548 by what?[16]
- The Temple of Diana (or Artemis) at Ephesus. Another very large building. Eratostratus burned it down so that his name would be remembered for ever, a ruse that appears not to have worked.
- The Pharos of Alexandria, a huge lighthouse built in about 280 BC. It could be seen from 42 miles away, or 20 feet in thick fog.
- The Statue of Zeus at Olympia. Built by Phidias in 433 BC. When he had it placed in the temple at Olympia, the sculptor prayed to Zeus to show him whether or not he approved of his work. A thunderbolt immediately hit the floor of the temple, but did no harm. (Phidias may or may not have been wearing rubber-soled shoes at the time.)
- The Mausoleum of Halicarnassus. This is the one everyone forgets. Cruel quizmasters may ask you to spell it correctly, too.

Currencies of the World

Usually a dinar. Or a dollar. Or a rupee. If not a franc, a quetzel, a cruzeiro or even a pound. There is a man in the pub tonight who knows all of these backwards. Why? Is he unhappy at home? Hasn't he anything better to do? The currency of Vietnam is the dong. Armenians prefer a dram. LSD, when it doesn't mean lysergic acid diethylamide 25, stands for *libra* (Latin for pound), *solidus* (shilling), *denarius* (penny). Cree

---

[16] The central tower of Lincoln Cathedral.

Indians once used pipes as their sole form of currency. Perhaps they knew something we don't.

Patron Saints and Saints' Days

Typical of the meat-and-potatoes general knowledge which is of no conceivable interest to anyone, yet still crops up in quizzes all the time. Only quizzers and Scotsmen remember that St Andrew's Day falls on 30 November. Only quizzers and members of the BNP remember that St George's Day is 23 April. Uruguay, rather greedily, has two saints (St Philip and St James, 1 May). Ireland must share St Patrick (17 March) with Nigeria. The US doesn't really have a patron saint at all, unless you count the Virgin Mary, who fills in for the Roman Catholics on 8 December. Perhaps St Ronald of Reagan could become the first divorced saint.

Meanwhile, virtually all jobs, medical conditions and character traits have their own patron saints, and hundreds of Catholic academics are working round the clock to fill the gaps. St Bibiana (2 December) is the patron saint of drinkers, while St Maurice (22 September) looks after dry cleaners. St Benedict (21 March) has potholers, while St Expeditus (19 April) doubles up for businessmen and learner drivers. St Nicholas (6 December) has perhaps the broadest portfolio, with responsibilities for children, choirboys, butchers, wine merchants (but not innkeepers), boatmen, pawnbrokers and most other merchants (although not tradesmen). St Bernardine of Siena (20 May) looks after advertising executives, possibly the shortest straw of all.

Warplanes and Tanks

Of residual interest to all blokes who used to make Airfix models as boys and still go dreamy at the mention of the word 'decals'. Unfortunately such people also regularly set pub quizzes, so it is useful to have one of them on your team if you can find one. He must remember about 5,000 different airplanes, know all the codewords for World War Two operations and be able to sing the theme to *The Dambusters* on demand. But make sure you just have the one. When two of these retards meet up, they drone on and on about guns and tanks until you nail their shoes to the floor, by which time the quiz is long since over and you have come third from last. One war bore is more than enough for most quiz teams, or lifetimes, come to that.

Inventions

Four full pages of the *Guinness Book of Answers* are taken up by lists of inventions, none of which you will be able to remember on the night. Never mind: what matters is that almost everything was invented years and years before you thought it was. The first operational helicopter goes back to 1909, the first cash register to 1879, the first dental plate to 1817. Even the compact disc is over twenty years old. Benjamin Franklin invented the lightning conductor, the rocking chair and the bifocal lens, and discovered the Gulf Stream. Thomas Alva Edison patented 1,093 inventions, including the phonograph and the electric lightbulb. Sir Arthur Sullivan had a lightbulb fitted on to the end of his baton by Edison so that he could conduct in the dark.

Roman Roads

Famously straight, and immensely irritating to all quizzers. Ermine Street ran north from London to York via the east Midlands. Watling Street ran north-west from London to the west Midlands, ending at Shrewsbury. Fosse Way, daringly, missed out London altogether, and crossed England from the coast in south Devon to a point south of Lincoln, where it joined Ermine Street. This, as far as most quizzes are concerned, was the extent of the Roman road system. Reports of tailbacks at Verulanium and a dropped load at Camulodunum should be disregarded.

Incidentally, beware of all questions that appear to demand the answer 'Hadrian's Wall'. According to new research, at least 78.8 per cent of them are trick questions, to which the correct answer is 'Antonine Wall'. Watch for the smug grin on the face of the quizmaster when he reads out the question again at the end of the round.

Food and Drink

If quizzers knew anything about food and drink they wouldn't be sitting in a smoky pub drinking thin gassy lager and wondering whether it's not too late for some overcooked 'pub grub' before the quiz starts. Any questions on the subject, therefore, are not so much going to skim the surface as miss it altogether. Which ingredient is added to a bechamel sauce to make a mornay sauce?[17] What term is used to describe a chicken that is cooked by being split down the middle and grilled?[18] Men, in particular, are apt to react with disgust to such questions, although they wouldn't say no to a few more chips. (Tomato ketchup? Thanks very much.)

The exception is curry, about which quizzers often know an awful lot. They know where balti dishes were first concocted,[19] they know which dish is the most popular in Britain,[20] some of them even know which spice produces that violent red sauce that ruins a white T-shirt for ever.[21] Such questions not only generate a sheaf of correct answers, they also tingle the

---

[17] Cheese.
[18] Spatchcocked.
[19] Birmingham.
[20] Chicken tikka masala.
[21] If it's not tartrazine, a food additive, it's often tinned tomato soup.

late-night tastebuds, with predictable wallet-emptying results. Any quizmaster who made a private deal with a local Indian restaurant to include the odd curry-oriented question could probably clean up.

Drink should be far more like home territory for most quizzers, but it causes many of the same problems. Questions on wine, for instance, are guaranteed to induce widespread panic, especially in a predominantly middle-class pub like the Prince of Wales where everyone likes to pretend they know more about wine than merely the difference between red and white. All you need to know, then, is very slightly more than everyone else, which may prove to be slightly more than nothing at all.

Real ale is the only danger area, as it often is in real life. Some quizmasters believe that happiness begins and ends with pint glasses full of murky liquid that smells like unwashed socks, and believe that everybody else should believe this too. If someone starts asking lots of dull questions about obscure Derbyshire breweries or 'ales' with names like Old Firepump, pour a glass of lager shandy over his head. He'll soon get the message.

Architecture

Doric, Ionic and Corinthian. Frank Lloyd Wright. John Nash, unless it was Inigo Jones. (Inigo Pipkin, by contrast, was the lead character in an early 1970s' children's TV show that also starred Hartley Hare, and has nothing to do with architecture at all.)

Phobias

Chris is proud of the number of phobias he remembers, although the one being asked always seems to have temporarily slipped his mind. In fact there are hundreds, most of which are crucifyingly boring. Blame Trivial Pursuit, one of whose landmark questions was 'Pogonophobia is the fear of what?'[22] This sent the insane and the disturbed scurrying into libraries to look up ever more abstruse examples, with the result that the *Guinness Book of Answers* now carries a two-page list of the buggers for easy reference. A few are straightforward. Thermophobia is the fear of heat, ecclesiaphobia is the fear of churches. The fear of syphilis, reassuringly, is syphilophobia. Others are ridiculous. Keraunothnetophobia is the fear of falling man-made satellites. Stasophobia is the fear of standing, while stasiphobia is the fear of standing upright. If you were terrified of the name Keith, you would suffer from onomatophobia. Phobophobics fear fear itself. And pantophobia is the fear of everything. (Not just the fear of pants.) There is no term, as yet, for the fear of quiz questions about phobias.

Technology

Nearly as terrifying as war bores are computer bores, who can usually be found in computer shops exchanging rib-tickling anecdotes about modems and baud rates. But where do they go after the computer shop shuts? Six nights of the week, of course, they go home and log on to porn on the Internet, but once a week they may push the boat out and congregate at some hapless pub quiz. There, if they are ever allowed to ask questions, they will reveal intimate knowledge of old computer games, how to hack into the Pentagon's war computers and the novels of Terry Pratchett. We usually set George on to them.

Incidentally, the first person ever to use a cashpoint machine in the United Kingdom was Reg Varney, star of *On the Buses*. It was at Barclays in Enfield, Middlesex, in 1967, and he was declaring it open at the time.

---

[22] Beards.

The Bible

Another source of frightening ignorance. Most people only ever see a Bible when they are in a hotel room, and even then they make sure to shove it right to the back of the drawer behind the porn stash and the just-in-case supply of prophylactics. (At least, so my businessmen friends assure me.) God's revenge, which is characteristically elegant, has been to inspire many wonderful quiz questions on the subject, which are guaranteed to catch out all quizzers who can't remember those large format all-colour collections of Bible stories we all read when we were six. In the book of Samuel: after stunning him with a slingshot, how did David finally kill Goliath?[23] Which religious group takes its name from a passage in the Old Testament, the book of Isaiah, chapter 43, verse 12?[24] According to Christian tradition, with which Latin phrase did St Peter greet Jesus when he met him on the Appian Way while Peter was fleeing from Rome?[25] All good stuff.

Other religions are just as fruitful, which at least prevents the occasional fight. Who, as mentioned in the title of a famous work of literature, is the Hindu god of love?[26] What is the world's oldest monotheistic faith (that is, belief in only one god)?[27] Rarely are questions asked about Islam, and I am not going to start here. No fatwa has yet been declared on a quizmaster, but it's probably only a matter of time.

---

[23] He cut off his head.

[24] Jehovah's Witnesses.

[25] 'Quo vadis?' See: The Classics.

[26] Kama. Around 50% per cent of teams always answer 'Sutra'.

[27] Judaism. Never forget to explain your terms, especially if they have five syllables.

Answers to Quiz 2

Human adults each have 206 bones; human babies are born with more (around 350, in fact). In 1903 Earl Russell queued all night to get the first ever car licence plate – which was A1. The European nation which was first to give women the vote and last in the Eurovision Song Contest most often was Finland. The writer of *Birds of the West Indies*, whose name was borrowed for a fictional character in a series of novels, was James Bond. Derek Jarman's *Sebastiane*, the only British film ever to be released in Britain with English subtitles, was filmed from beginning to end in Latin.

Quiz 3

- What hardly ever happen in Hertford, Hereford and Hampshire?
- Who is Lord Marmaduke Bunkerton better known as?
- Which football team is theoretically entitled to enter both the FA Cup and the Welsh Cup as their stadium is half in England and half in Wales, though they now play exclusively in the FA Cup competition?
- Which real life character appears in all of the following works of fiction: *The Negotiator* by Frederick Forsyth, *XPD* by Len Deighton, *Titmuss Regained* by John Mortimer and *The Child in Time* by Ian McEwan?
- Do zebras have white stripes or black stripes?

9

A Quiz Childhood

*'In a television programme on schools, some elderly
viewers were amused to see a master in class throw a
coloured balloon into the air and invite his pupils to
describe its appearance as it came down. "Is this
education?" some of those viewers asked.'*

(Editorial in *Look and Learn*, 3 November 1962)

Most quizzers start young. 'Dad! Dad!' we would scream, as
our fathers sped through city traffic. 'Did you know there are
more sheep in New Zealand than people?' All fathers knew
there were more sheep in New Zealand than people, because
we had told them so at least twenty times already. A good fact
was like a good story: it only improved with repetition. 'Dad!
Dad! Did you know an oyster can survive up to four months
out of water?' 'Not if you eat it first,' Dad would mumble, narrowly missing a pedestrian.

Children gobble up facts, and then regurgitate them over
and over again. This always seems to come as a surprise to
parents; you can only feel sorry for them. Babies pass the
projectile vomiting stage, and parents think they are in the
clear. But before long the little ones are talking, and about
half an hour later they are asking complex and often unanswerable questions that all start with the word 'Why?' From
there it's a short step to sentences beginning 'Did you
know . . .', and a tidal wave of facts that overwhelms all other

conversation. Soon parents are looking back at the old gunk-on-the-shoulder days with real fondness. It's at moments like these that some couples, united by madness, look each other in the eye and say, 'Let's have another one.' Which means, 'Let's have one that doesn't say anything.' Thus the human race propagates, bringing a new meaning to the phrase 'the facts of life'.

Several decades later the same fact-crazed kids are going to pub quizzes and wondering why they have so many brothers and sisters. It's quite normal for adults to forget what it was like to be a child, for if they did remember how ghastly and boring and frustrating it was, they would never have any themselves. As it is, the process of forgetting starts young. Most of us, as children, spend a disproportionate amount of time looking forward to not being children. We aspire to the next stage up, and reject all that seems to us babyish or immature. So as we learn, we also carefully unlearn. We embrace new experiences and quietly forget old ones. Some people manage to forget that they had ever been children at all, and go on to enjoy fruitful careers in politics, the City and organised crime. The rest of us reach adulthood, or what we imagine to be adulthood, in a state of almost total confusion.

The answers, clearly, lie in these forgotten childhoods. Psychotherapists, who have fifty minutes to kill before they can ask for their fee, always start with childhood, and usually stay there as long as possible. They believe that behaviour patterns are set in our earliest years, and can only be understood after years of therapeutic work (all major credit cards accepted). This seems fair enough, until you realise that to get at these answers, you need to ask some awkward questions. Was everything all right at home? Did your parents love and nurture you? Or did they beat you with staves and tie you to your bed with piano wire? Did they lock the only useful encyclopaedia in the rat-infested basement? Would they let you watch *Screen Test*, with Michael Rodd?

This is deep and dark territory for us all. It's hard enough waking up in the middle of the night sweating and shouting without having to do it during the day as well. Quizzers can only wonder at the terrible childhood traumas that lurk behind their desire to put everything in alphabetical order. This instinct towards ritual and routine, the sheer visceral hunger for bonus points, the mad-eyed fury when you're convinced the questionmaster has got it wrong again: are these the marks of a sane and well-adjusted adult?

Having thought and argued about it for years, and having ignored my girlfriend's increasingly strident suggestions that I seek psychiatric help, I have come to the conclusion that they are. Ritual and routine are the cornerstones of civilised behaviour, and the occasional display of irrational rage never did anyone any harm. Quizzing seems no madder than any other leisure pursuit. Indeed, compared to some of them – jogging, S&M, organised religion – it stands out as a beacon of sanity in a palpably barmy world.

Quizzing, at heart, is an innocent activity. Far from masking our forgotten childhoods, it unwittingly taps straight into them. That inner swot I mentioned earlier roars to the surface, and for a few happy hours we are eight years old again. Do we know that there are more sheep in New Zealand than there are people? Yes, we do, and with luck we will know it for the rest of our lives.

If quizzing is innocent, it's because most quizzers grew up in more innocent times. This is no mere nostalgia. As our national culture has mutated and coarsened, the texture of childhood has changed irrevocably. It's hard for even a youngish adult to digest just how much has been lost. Those of us who reached sentience in the 1960s, for instance, would have enjoyed at least one of the following:

- *Look and Learn* magazine.
- The I-SPY Club.
- Access to a well-stocked library.
- Regular viewings of *Blue Peter* and/or *Magpie*, and associated crush on Lesley Judd/Susan Stranks/Peter Purves.

True, even at the time, these were not exactly the most hard-boiled of childhood pursuits. We played football and threw each other off railway bridges like all the other kids, because we had to show how hard and streetwise we were, even if we weren't. But the swot within us also wanted to get good reports and pass exams. When we looked through the *Encyclopaedia Britannica*, it was for more than photographs of naked African women with dangly breasts. (Although obviously we knew those particular page numbers by heart.) Our hunger for facts was intense. To make sure that we consumed the sort of facts they wanted us to consume, many parents edged us none too subtly in the direction of *Look and Learn*.

A publication like *Look and Learn* is impossible to imagine today. There were no comic strips, at least in the early years. No jokes, in any form we would now recognise. Most courageously of all, there was a complete absence of gratuitous violence. Parents and teachers approved strongly of *Look and Learn*. Like All-Bran, they thought it would be good for us in the long run. Thirty years later, fibrous breakfast cereals are still with us. Fibrous children's magazines have long since died out.

A year or two ago Michael, one of my team-mates at the Cock Tavern, found some battered binders full of old *Look and Learn*s in a junk shop. He dragged home as many as he could carry. Each one is fascinating – a time capsule between hard covers. Every week you could read scholarly articles about history and geography and science and coin collecting, all illustrated with sober line drawings and photographs of the surprisingly elderly hacks who worked on the magazine. The byline pic of Peter Duncan, *Look and Learn's* 'roving reporter' (any word or phrase coined after 1850 was invariably placed in inverted commas), showed a man infinitely older than anyone we had ever met, although he was probably only about forty-five. Regular columns included Pioneers of the Faith ('This week, Mission to Burma by the Rev. J M Poe') and The World of Stamps ('Historic Issues From the Vatican City by C W Hill'). 'Special series' would deal with issues of burning significance to the ambitious eleven-year-old ('What Do You Want to Be? Our special series on careers by Joan Llewelyn Owens. This week, the Civil Service'). Sometimes it seemed as though the editorial staff were actively considering self-parody ('Man of the Week: St Anthony of Padua, 1195–1231'). In reality, the magazine's earnestness was invulnerable. Only *Look and Learn* could have published a double-page spread on a Belgian village festival at which everyone dressed up as giant shrimps. The piece, headlined 'Honouring the Humble Shrimp', contained not the tiniest hint that anyone might find such behaviour at all funny.

No *Look and Learn*, though, was complete without its quiz. This was deemed a vital component of the magazine's editorial mix – so vital, in fact, that for a brief and glorious spell it even graced the front cover. Some of the questions posed we would struggle to answer today. One of the most gifted English novelists was born in Yorkshire in 1816. What was her name?[1] How many gold medals did Britain win in the 1964 Olympic Games?[2] In Shakespeare's play *Macbeth*, what wood moved

---

[1] Charlotte Brontë.
[2] Five.

towards which hill?[3] None of them straightforward, and all from the issue of 20 May 1967, price 1s. 3d.

The magazine simply assumed that its readers were eager to learn. Compromise with the dark forces of entertainment was not even contemplated. Editorials, in particular, did not give an inch. 'Lynn, a Birmingham reader, asks a question of only four words. But what a difficult one it is to answer! Lynn wants to know, what is good art?' So began the editorial of 21 July 1962, which went on to explain, with admirable lack of self-consciousness, exactly what good art was and how you could recognise it. The following week's column raised an even more controversial subject. 'Do you think that your parents are "squares"? And if so, do you agree that one day your children will say the same about you?'

Curiously, this intellectual rigour was rarely reflected in the letters column. Readers realised early that only questions that were easy to answer were likely to be accepted for publication. On 28 July 1962 John Davies of Ipswich asked 'Who invented the telephone?' and won a 15 shillings Post Office Savings Gift Token. Had he really wanted to know he could have looked it up or asked a teacher – but how much more satisfying it must have been to see your name printed on page 2 of *Look and Learn*. In the same issue George Barnes of Banbury asked how the Red Sea got its name. *Look and Learn* told him. 'The colour of its water sometimes appears red. Actually this colouring is due to the presence in the water of vast numbers of minute red-coloured plants.' This was presumably a proud moment for George Barnes of Banbury. Thirty-five years later he takes part in a pub quiz. 'How does the Red Sea get its name?' asks the questionmaster. Somewhere in the back of George's mind, a long-buried

---

[3] Birnam Wood towards Dunsinane Hill.

memory quietly stirs. Too quietly, as it turns out. 'No, haven't got a clue,' he says. 'Whose round is it?'

Look and Learn, astonishingly, lasted over twenty years: its last edition was published as late as March 1982. But the robust didacticism of its early years had long since been diluted. In 1967 the action comic *Ranger* had been incorporated as a pull-out supplement, introducing readers to the delights of Jason January Space Cadet, Dan Dakota Lone Gun and, of course, The Trigan Empire, a space opera of legendary complexity and innumerable explosions. Even *Look and Learn* could not survive without gratuitous violence for ever. And yet the magazine's readers still knew which side their bread was buttered. From a 1968 issue: 'Dear Sir, I was very interested in the "Nile Expedition" in *Look and Learn* No. 271. My grandfather was in the relief force for General Gordon, and he held all the medals from the expedition, which we now possess. Yours, Ronald Gauld (age 11), Aberdeen.'

Ronald, I think we can assume, would have been an enthusiastic member of the I-SPY Club. This powerful organisation operated from the offices of a succession of Fleet Street newspapers, and taught tinies everything they would ever know about moths, steam trains and wild flowers. When I mentioned the subject of this chapter to a friend of mine (now an eminent newspaper executive), he started rambling on about the 30 points he had once scored for sighting a foxglove. He had been an army child, growing up on bleak military bases where anything resembling a wild flower was hunted down and exterminated with lethal nerve poisons. But he had not given up. Armed with his I-SPY Wild Flowers handbook (1/-), he had searched most of the surrounding countryside before no. 38, Foxglove, appeared before him like the Holy Grail. 'All parts of this plant are poisonous,' he read. 'Another name for it is Dead Men's Bells.' I know he read this because I recently came across the same I-SPY handbook in a second-hand bookshop. Sadly, memory had played another of its cruel tricks. Simon had never forgotten his foxglove, but he had forgotten that it was worth only 20 points – no big deal in I-SPY terms. Inflation affects everything in the end, even childhood reminiscence.

If it were still going, the I-SPY Club would probably now be considered rather sinister. Big Chief I-SPY, a shadowy figure who we all thought had a lot in common with Ernst Stavro Blofeld, wrote his column every day in a style both triumphalist and strangely impenetrable. One day he would record 'I-SPY triumphs in tracking and spotting.' To the GREAT TRIBE (very fond of capital letters was Big Chief I-SPY) he sent secret messages and passwords in code. 'In his unique way he manages to set everyone I-SPYing.' You could have said the same about the KGB.

Joining the tribe, sorry, TRIBE, was easy. 'Ask your newsagent to show you the I-SPY Membership Packet.' (Not something you would risk nowadays.) If the newsagent was out of stock, you could send the Tribal Fee – one shilling, plus 4d. postage – to Big Chief I-SPY himself at Wigwam-by-the-Water, 4 Upper Thames Street, London EC4 (the address changed frequently for security reasons). Soon you too would be wandering the countryside with your I-SPY booklets, desperately looking for natterjack toads, corn dollies and someone who might feasibly come from Nigeria. There were I-SPY books about cars and aircraft, birds and trees, churches, pets and insects. More ambitious titles included Antique Furniture, Everyday Machines and On The Pavement, which was a particular disappointment, as the one thing you could be sure of seeing on the pavement never scored you any points at all.

The I-SPY books recorded a disappearing world. Number 27 in the series, Country Crafts, included a page on Making Bricks By Hand (40 points) and asked you to find a Travelling

Tinker in the act of Re-Seating a Chair or Riveting China (35 points each). And yet they were utterly addictive. The idea that you could score points simply by spotting things and writing them down in your notebook was impossible to resist. If you scored 1,250 points, you qualified for Second Class Honours, which meant you could fill in the mock certificate at the back of your I-SPY booklet and get it signed by your parents. Accumulate 1,500 points and Big Chief would award you First Class Honours, and send you off to a special spying school near Minsk. At least, that's what we had all heard: no one I knew ever achieved First Class Honours without blatantly cheating. (When Michael's parents discovered that he had made up some of his sightings, they refused to let him send his booklet in.) Nonetheless, we were probably the last generation who took I-SPY even remotely seriously. The club stuttered on into the late 1980s, when David Bellamy briefly and rather bizarrely became the first Big Chief I-SPY to reveal his identity (in the past Parliament had not even officially acknowledged the post's existence). It probably did well to survive so long: no childhood pursuit that relied only on honesty and a desire to accumulate knowledge would have much of a chance today.

If the rain fell, which it invariably did from the first day of the summer holiday to the first day back at school in September, the embryonic quizzer might go round to someone else's house and play a game. Magic Robot was made by Merit and believed to be the greatest and most miraculous children's game of them all, at least for the half-hour it took you to work out how it was done. Question and answer sheets, of which there were far too few, came with two circular holes cut out in the middle. Questions surrounded one hole, answers the other. Slotting a sheet over two metal protruberances, both ingeniously magnetised, you would select a question with your metallic pointer and the Magic Robot, placed on the other magnet, would rotate briefly before pointing out the correct answer. 'Wow!' you said, even though the fact thus illustrated interested you not at all. What mattered was that the Magic Robot knew all the answers. After a while, though, you realised that there was a pattern to the Magic Robot's brilliance. Studying its behaviour more closely, you noticed that it always pointed to the answer positioned eight notches around the circle from the equivalent question. The Magic Robot didn't know the answers after all. It could just count up to eight. This was not half as exciting, so you packed the Magic Robot away in its box and, as you would with Trivial Pursuit twenty years later, put it on the top of your wardrobe for ever. If there had been child therapists at the time, Magic Robot Trauma would have been written up in all the textbooks and eventually turned into the subject of a six-part documentary series on Channel 4. As it is, only the discovery that the Mouse Trap game never worked caused our generation more grief and distress.

Several years later, after the fuss had died down, Merit ingeniously repackaged the game as Confucius He Say, and proceeded to traumatise a new generation. By then, fortunately, most of us had moved on. Having been bitten by the quizzing bug – an especially vicious little insect, I always thought – we were constantly on the lookout for ever more challenging and obscure sources of meaningless information. Quiz questions became a way of attracting our attention. The Pied Piper of Hamelin only had a flute; think what he might have accomplished with an encyclopaedia. The wise heads at Trebor knew this, and so in the late 1960s the Quiz Bar was launched, to flourish for a few short years until Curly Wurlys came in and changed the face of confectionery for good. Trebor's Quiz Bar offered not just a sweet rectangular chew of radioactive hue and intestine-dissolving acidity, it also had a quiz question temptingly displayed on its wrapper. You handed over your 3d (or perhaps 1½p). You carefully ripped open the wrapper. And inside, as well as the chew, would be the answer to the question, printed on the wrapper's waxy interior. If you had had the same question before – and there were not that many to go round – you might be able to bet a gullible classmate that you knew the answer. There might have been more foolproof methods of augmenting your income as an eight-year-old, but I never found them.

Do your homework, read *Look and Learn*, pay attention, wear a neat blazer, speak a little like Trevor Howard and Celia Johnson in *Brief Encounter* – and you might, if you were very well behaved, be invited to represent your school in *Top of the Form*. This was the apotheosis of the Quiz Childhood, a peak from which a whole world of achievement and excellence could be surveyed, a peak from which the only way was down. How we sneered at the bespectacled goody-goodies who lined up in well-scrubbed foursomes to be asked questions by Geoffrey Wheeler. How we wished it was us up there instead.

The show began on the BBC's Light Programme, and continued on Radio 2 long after its dangerous television spin-off had been abandoned as old hat. Richard Dimbleby was an early questionmaster, orotund and avuncular, before being replaced in the early 1960s by Wheeler and Paddy Feeny. Each would present his half of the show from a different school, the two being connected by a land line, which for the BBC in the 1960s was about as technologically advanced as the Apollo space mission. Each school hall sounded equally draughty, and each school team sounded equally posh. All contestants were eager to show off their knowledge of world currencies and improper fractions. In the right circumstances the show could have incited a socialist revolution by itself.

TV Top Of The Form began in 1962, slimmed down to a single location and a single presenter in Geoffrey Wheeler.

Although he was as neatly blazered as anyone could be, it was his parting that truly set the tone. Ramrod straight, and clearly visible on 405 lines, it embodied the show's upper-middlebrow, middle-to-upper-middle-class, unashamedly didactic ethos. He was younger then than I am now – far younger. He also managed to be older and more responsible than many of us will ever be. It is curious that, while many famous and accomplished people have happily admitted that they were once on *University Challenge*, no one has ever owned up to appearing on *TV Top of the Form*. This may be because all the thousands of little swots who took part during its thirteen long years of transmission went on to lives of unremitting drab mediocrity. Alternatively it may just have been the most embarrassing TV programme of all time. By comparison, even *Ask the Family* was cool.

Where did this all lead? In time, all the usual things: slightly disappointing exam results, post-adolescent rebellion, the grim nonfulfilment of adult life, botched suicide attempts in suburban garages. So much promise unrealised, as it always is. Nonetheless, *Look and Learn*, I-SPY, Magic Robot, Trebor's Quiz Bar and *TV Top of the Form* formed the cultural hinterland of an entire generation. They were the sensible, vaguely bookish pursuits that most bourgeois parents would have been keen to thrust upon their idle offspring. And now? Thirty years later all we can do to stave off the boredom is go to a pub quiz every Tuesday evening. Perhaps we should have gone out and played football a little more often.

Answers to Quiz 3

Hurricanes hardly ever happen in Hertford, Hereford and Hampshire, according to the song in *My Fair Lady*. Lord Marmaduke Bunkerton was better known, to generations of

Beano readers, as Lord Snooty. The football team that is theoretically entitled to enter both the FA Cup and the Welsh Cup is Chester City. The real life character who appeared in novels by Frederick Forsyth, Len Deighton, John Mortimer and Ian McEwan was Margaret Thatcher. And zebras have white stripes (on a black background).

Quiz 4

- What colour is the flight recorder in aeroplanes?
- In which Shakespeare tragedy does a Roman general, driven mad by the murder of his two sons, kill the sons of the wife of the Emperor and serve them to her in a pie?
- Which is the coldest capital city in the world? (Temperatures there regularly reach −35° Centigrade.)
- What did Pink Floyd sing about once, Liza Minnelli sing about twice and Abba sing about three times?
- What does this sequence of letters represent: ATGCLVLSSCAP?

10
Playing the Game

'If a thing is worth doing, it is worth doing badly.'

(G K Chesterton)

There is one simple way to make sure you win every quiz you enter: know everything. This is Kevin Ashman's chosen method, and so far it has helped him win *Mastermind, Brain of Britain, Fifteen-To-One* (series 3 in 1989) and countless lesser trophies. Chris, who, as our gnarled quizzing veteran, may have spent one weekend too many in grim banqueting suites in drab hotels competing in vain for uninspiring prizes against teams of greasy-haired men wearing the shirt of Division 2 football teams, has come up against Kevin Ashman on several occasions. Each one, he says, is seared on to his consciousness. Even I saw him once, in just such a banqueting suite in just such a hotel. He was sitting at a table with five identical-looking men of indeterminate age. All were wearing sweaters only mothers could have knitted. As soon as I saw them, I knew we were out of our league.

It was our team's first (and so far only) foray into the wilder margins of quiz life. Chris was there, of course, as were George, Terence, George's girlfriend Lesley and an old friend

of mine called Richard, who had been a regular at The
Wrestlers and would soon move to the West Country to
escape events like these. Many of the other teams had come
from far away, but they all seemed to know each other,
exchanging formal nods of recognition in the only echo of our
altogether gentler contests at the Prince of Wales. They also
came in more extreme shapes and sizes than we were used to.
Some were death-defyingly thin. One or two were tall and
thin, with Adam's apples like ping pong balls. Many were
strikingly overweight. Indeed, a few tables from us sat some of
the fattest people any of us had ever seen.

It's funny: once you have noticed something like that, it's
impossible to unnotice it. 'How did they get that fat?' asked
Terence. 'By eating a lot,' said George. They looked hungry
now, even though it was only half an hour since lunch. 'Quick,
hide the Rolos,' said Chris. But the fatties were not interested
in our feeble sweetmeats. They had other ideas. On a trestle
table by the far wall, concealed under a sheet, were the sandwiches that were obviously intended as our half-time snack.
The fatties eyed them up as a lion eyes up a gazelle. In an
hour or so the sheet would be removed and the sandwiches
would become generally available. The fatties could not bear
the thought of this. They wanted them all to themselves. They
were literally sweating with greed.

We were mesmerised. 'There are only five of them,' said
Terence. Teams of six were the norm. 'Perhaps one of them is
sitting on two chairs,' said George. 'I think you'll find they're
all sitting on two chairs,' said Chris. 'Hang on,' said George,
'isn't there someone else in there? Look, just behind the one in
the dungarees, darting in and out of the shadows?' Indeed
there was. They had brought a thin person along too.
Presumably he was there to do the things they couldn't do,
like walk. Later on, when the sandwiches were finally
unveiled, the thin person was sent off to fill some plates. A

minute or so later, he was sent off to fill them again. At the same time anxious phone calls were being made on a fatty's mobile. Twenty minutes later a motorcycle messenger arrived, carefully balancing five large pizza boxes and enough garlic bread to feed Rwanda. This team were much more entertaining than the quiz, which included a full round of questions about gardening. Kevin Ashman's team won by miles. We came 19th.

If you are going to know everything, you cannot allow yourself to be distracted by humorous fat people, or questions you don't like, or anything really. How many of us are willing to make this sacrifice? On the train on the way up I had sat opposite just such a quizzer, who in preparation for the day's entertainment was poring over a book of facts. It would be hard to exaggerate the intensity of concentration with which he studied his text. I doubt even derailment would have distracted him. And yet what was the point of revising for a quiz? If you don't know it by now, you never will: years of exam disappointment teach us that, if nothing else. But the quiz ascetic, who yearns to know all that there is to know, cares not what the outside world thinks of him – probably doesn't even notice, in fact. He certainly didn't give any sign of noticing me. I, the sad anal retentive, looked at him, the even sadder, possibly mildly autistic anal retentive rocking backwards and forwards in his train seat, and I felt pity, tinged with mild contempt. Later on, when he and his team came third or fourth or wherever, and we were still gawping at fat people, he might have looked at me in much the same way.

The gravest risk of wanting to know everything is that the pleasure in competing gradually seeps away. Omniscience requires such work and dedication that the notion of having a good time is bound to be marginalised. You sometimes see a pub team who have become, if anything, too proficient for their own good. They have grown used to winning; they probably expect to win. After a while they no longer show pleasure when they get an answer right. They don't cheer, and they wouldn't even contemplate triumphalist high fives. Instead they just nod seriously, as though any display of emotion might be interpreted by their rivals as a sign of weakness. Mr Spock had to undergo the ancient and mystical Vulcan rite of Kohlinar to purge his mind of all emotion. If he had been a member of an over-serious pub quiz team, he probably needn't have bothered.

Such matter-of-factness has its uses. Teams who take correct answers for granted can convince other teams that they are invincible, which is the next best thing to actually being invincible. But watch out. If you can't enjoy your correct answers – even the ones at which you arrived through ridiculous good fortune – then soon you will begin to fear wrong ones. You will become to resent every small failure. Maybe you will decide that you don't know enough. Perhaps you would feel safer knowing everything. From there it's a short step to sitting in a train on your way to a quiz rocking backwards and forwards reading a book of facts. Every time I see him in my mind's eye, I shudder. But then if I didn't think I were capable of such behaviour myself, I probably wouldn't see him in my mind's eye at all.

So much, then, for knowing everything. Most of us, conscious of these terrible consequences, learn to live with our imperfection. We know we shall never know all the answers, but so what? What count are the answers we do know, and particularly the ones we dredge up from some dark recess of memory at the last moment when all hope had seemed lost. As in sport, as in life, so in quiz: our main duty is to play to our potential, to make the most of such talents as we have. From time to time, as in sport, as in life, you will be immoderately lucky. You will guess wildly and get every question right. Your judgement will be flawless. Team-mates will defer to you. Terence will voluntarily buy you a drink. Your adrenal glands will pump like pistons, and steam will pour from your ears. It will be Your Evening. Enjoy it: you may never experience the like of it again.

At other times luck deserts you and you forget everything. On such an evening you will amaze yourself with the number of different ways you can get things wrong. Your team-mates will forgive you in time, but for this evening your best bet is to keep your mouth shut, or perhaps feign serious illness during the bonus round. Nothing you will do tonight will be right. Indeed, your first and most serious mistake was to turn up.

Most of the time, happily, you are neither genius nor cretin, and must make your own luck. What is required could probably be called 'technique' if it didn't boil down to plain common sense. Playing a pub quiz is like playing any game or sport: talent is useful but temperament is vital. The beauty of this game is that everyone has a chance. With a clear mind and an empty bladder you can achieve far more than you ever thought yourself capable of. Any team can win if it wants to. Ignorance is no barrier to glory. First prize tonight could be within your grasp. Repeat this mantra every eighteen seconds:

> *The winning team is not necessarily the team that knows the most: it's the team that gives the most correct answers.*

Empty your mind, with lager if necessary. Bond with your team-mates. Concentrate with all your heart, and don't admit defeat, unless of course you score fewer points than one of the other teams. And never forget: you don't need to know everything. Nearly everything will do.

Leadership

Someone must hold the pen: that is clear. Chances are, also, that there will be someone who desperately wants to hold the

pen. In a team laden with potential leaders, however, there
may be several people who desperately want to hold the pen.
This can create procedural problems, spill drinks and generate
social tension, but there's no need to fret. Sit back and let
Darwinism sort out the mess. Survival of the Most Arrogant is
the general rule, and the person who shouts loudest (usually
male, by virtue of testicle ownership and powerful lungs) will
almost always prevail. In fact it doesn't matter who holds the
pen, as long as he is decisive and willing to take the blame for
all wrong decisions. If he finds this responsibility too onerous
he will soon develop incurable writers' cramp ('My doctor says
it's repetitive strain injury and I mustn't even hold a pen for
eight months'), and someone more suited to the role can take
over.

Team Size

The more players in your team, the more likely you are to
win . . . or so it seems when a couple of your mates have not
turned up and the next table is groaning with intellectual
muscle. In the Prince of Wales we imposed a limit of six
players per team after one bunch repeatedly won with nine or
ten. Not only did they take all the money, they also had a
great time. Each Tuesday seemed like a mini-reunion of old
friends who enjoyed each other's company enormously. So we
put a stop to that and they never came again.

In fact a team of seven, eight or nine will often be more
trouble than it's worth. If you all love each other deeply, and
can subsume your egos to the common good, then you have no
place on a quiz team, which needs everyone at their sharpest
and most aggressive. When an oversized team does well, it's
usually because half of them are only there for the chat and
the company. Only a handful will actually be doing the quiz.
If all eight or nine try to take part, you will get more difficult
questions right than you otherwise would have – everyone

knows something the others don't know – but you may not realise it, as there will be so many different suggestions for each answer it will be impossible to sort out which is the right one. The power struggles in oversized teams are complex and all-consuming, leaving little energy for the winning of quizzes. Far more sensible to split the team into two smaller outfits, which can then compete with each other to the death.

The optimum size for a quiz team is probably four, although some people swear by five. Anything more creates unnecessary strife, while anything less punctures huge holes in your combined knowledge. All three of you will know everything there is to know about the films of John Carpenter, but nothing about, say, geography. Fielding a team of just two is pure optimism. One regular team at the Prince of Wales, who trade under the title 'Chris and John' (these being their names), slog away every week, even though the two of them seem to know exactly the same things. If you set a quiz knee-deep in history, geography and the classics, they are unassailable, but a single question on popular culture always undoes them. Fortunately they are old friends and infinitely patient. They know their day will come, sometime in the distant future when quizmasters come to their senses and stop setting questions about *Emmerdale*.

If you are by yourself, you really are asking for trouble. See 'Singletons'.

Second Guessing

There is one cast-iron rule of quizzing, which is as follows:

The first answer you think of is usually the right one.

Unfortunately there is a corollary to this rule:

Sometimes it's not.

Most quizzes are won and lost by people second-guessing themselves. The question is read out and immediately an answer
comes into your mind. You tell your team-mates. They may
greet this answer with enthusiasm, if not ecstasy, or they may
be sceptical. Someone who knows less about the subject than
you do may have an alternative answer. Or perhaps you yourself begin to think too hard, and consider too many alternatives.
The second answer sounds more and more convincing. Soon
you have absolutely no idea which one is right. You have
answer A in your head, and floating a little way away from it,
answer B, but no thought processes connect either of these
answers to each other or the working portion of your mind. You
lose all sense of proportion. Maybe you start to drool. Your
team-mates, meanwhile, have lost all confidence in you. After
an endless circular argument, everyone agrees, more positively
than any of them feel, that the second answer is right. It isn't.
You have wasted time and energy considering two answers
when the first answer you thought of was right all along. You
are furious with yourself, and your team-mates are furious with
you. 'Why weren't you a bit more forceful?' asks the most
forceful of them. The first answer, the right answer, now seems
blindingly obvious, as indeed, with hindsight, it always did.

Don't worry about it. Everyone does this all the time.
Second-guessing yourself is an occupational hazard of thinking
at all. The more quizzes you go to, the more likely you are to
do it. One week the Prince of Wales quiz was easier than
usual, and we knew that if we wanted to win we couldn't
afford to make a single mistake. So we made loads. One question asked how Tsar Ivan IV of Russia was better known. 'Ivan
the Terrible, of course,' said Terence, who failed Russian A
level a long time ago. 'Ah, but is it?' the rest of us wondered.
Could this be an ingenious double bluff? The other famous
Ivan was Ivan the Great: it might be him. Ivan the Terrible
was far too obvious an answer. Easy as the quiz was, surely it

couldn't be that easy. 'Perhaps it's a double bluff,' said Chris. 'Perhaps it's so obvious that it can't be Ivan the Terrible that it is Ivan the Terrible after all.' After long debate we decided it was a triple bluff, and wrote down 'Ivan the Great'. Every other team in the pub wrote 'Ivan the Terrible', which was the right answer.

Assertiveness

Even among old friends, in a comfortable, boozy environment, a lack of assertiveness can fatally undermine your individual performance. You think you know the answer, but you say nothing, either because (a) you don't want to take the blame if the answer turns out to be wrong, (b) other more assertive figures in your team are certain they know the answer, although you know they know nothing about anything and would struggle to tie their own shoelaces, or because (c) you are so busy making neat lists of things in your head, labelled (a), (b) and (c) that you have lost all concentration and can't remember what the question was anyway. To which the only possible answer is: pull yourself together and stop whingeing. Did you really expect any sympathy?

The Expert

The Expert will not be denied. He knows the answer to this question. He knew it immediately. His certainty is contagious. Nuremberg rallies would not doubt him. The only problem is that *you* know he is wrong. It may be a genuine and unforeseen error on his part, or he may be an arrogant moron. Some people find it much easier to be certain than to be right. They can cause havoc on quiz teams. I knew this fellow who so needed the respect of his team-mates that he turned every such incident into a test of that respect – in short, love me, love my answer, even though it is wrong. His team house-trained him eventually, but not without pain, recriminations and countless lost points.

How you deal with an Expert is up to you. Chris would recommend patience, while George might suggest something involving a smashed pint glass. Team-mates have to trust each other. (Failing that, not actively wanting to murder each other will usually do.)

Blanks

We all have our subjects about which we know nothing. Even they who seek to know everything know nothing about something. It's a matter of finding out what, and William G Stewart, for some reason, has a particular talent for this. One of the regular pleasures of *Fifteen-To-One* is watching the come-uppance of know-all Grand Finalists who can recite the *Aeneid* in Latin, and know that the chemical formula for sugar is $C_{12}H_{22}O_{11}$, but look blank when the words 'Cilla Black' are mentioned. Some general knowledge is just too general for such people. Out they go, beaten by some nice old geezer in a strobing check jacket who knew less but had more luck. There ain't no justice – which seems fair enough.

As a normal, hypersensitive individual I used to feel oddly ashamed when confronted by my own ignorance of certain subjects – as though knowing nothing about horse racing was my fault, rather than, of course, horse racing's. Other personal voids include botany (plants and flowers: love looking at them, don't know what any of them are) and poetry (at smarter quizzes I feign unconsciousness). Whenever a question was asked on one of these subjects I would pretend to concentrate hard as though trying to think of an answer. Whereas what I was really concentrating on was looking as though I was concentrating. All very silly, and metaphysically exhausting after a while.

Then I noticed the way George reacted to questions about his particular knowledge vacuum, the cinema. George has a wonderful general knowledge, based on his genuine interest in a broad variety of subjects, assisted by a naturally retentive memory and fired by the feral urge to beat those bloody complaining actors who always sit at the next table. But he is not interested in films: never sees them, 'can't be arsed', he says. It's a significant gap; questions on the subject crop up all the time. And when they do, George just shrugs his shoulders and says, 'Haven't a clue.' It's almost a boast. He displays his ignorance for all to see, and cares not what people think. 'Haven't a clue' – or, if someone asks more than once, 'Haven't the foggiest'. In the bubbling cauldron of the pub quiz, these are brave words indeed.

Singletons

This is primarily a social dilemma. You have turned up to the quiz, and no one else on your team is there. Are they late? Did you forget to confirm by phone? Did they all tell you they couldn't come and you have forgotten? Have they all gone on holiday and failed to tell you? These and more questions race through your mind. Do they not want to be on the same team as you any more? (In the background, you are vaguely aware of the quizmaster asking the first question of round one.) Perhaps they have all gone on holiday together: that's why no one said anything. Are they all right? Have their cars broken down? Have they been eaten by leopards? Or are they all just working late? Has there been some disaster at home? At all their homes?

You sit alone on your bar stool.

You are very conscious that you are by yourself.

You sip your drink.

Everybody can hear you sip (they can't). Everybody is deliberately not looking at you. You have no mates.

(Actually no one gives a monkeys. They are all too busy doing the quiz.)

Come on, come on, you unreliable bastards.

Right, I'm staying five minutes more and that's it.

But if I leave before the quiz is over, it will look as though I'm leaving early because I have no mates. (Which I will be, of course.)

Shall I do the quiz by myself? I'll come last because I am not paying attention and have no mates.

Just walk through the door, someone, anyone. Damn and damn and damn you all, you shits, you bastards.

Or shall I try to join one of the other regular teams, who will be terribly kind and painfully polite and think that I have no mates? Because they will be that and they will think that, and if my team-mates do eventually arrive I'll have to decide whether to stay with my new team-mates or go back to my old team-mates . . .

(By this time it's halfway through round two and you are more than halfway to a coronary thrombosis. It's for this reason, among others, that the most common greeting you will hear between friends at a pub quiz is 'And where the fuck have you been?' Next time check someone else is turning up before you set out.)

(There is an alternative nightmare: thinking they will turn up, entering anyway – and winning by yourself. Chris did this once at the Victoria, another Highgate pub. He was too embarrassed to collect his prize. George did it too, at the same pub, when Chris failed to turn up. George, of course, was exultant, and hopped up to claim his winnings with a huge smug grin on his face. How he escaped unharmed remains one of North London's more enduring mysteries.)

Answers to Quiz 4

The flight recorder in aeroplanes is bright orange. (It's called a Black Box because it's named after someone called Black.)

The Roman general who, driven mad by the murder of his two sons, kills the sons of the wife of the Emperor and serves them to her in a pie is Titus Andronicus. The world's coldest capital city is Ulan Bator in Mongolia. Pink Floyd sang 'Money', Liza Minnelli sang 'Money Money', Abba sang 'Money Money Money'. And the sequence ATGCLVLSS-CAP represents the signs of the zodiac: Aries, Taurus, Gemini, Cancer . . .

Quiz 5

- Goal shooter, goal attack, wing attack, centre, wing defence, goal defence and goalkeeper are the seven playing positions in which sport?
- Colonel Paul W Tibbets was a decorated US bomber pilot in World War Two, but his mother's name is better remembered today. What was her name?
- What was located on the island of Isla Nublar?
- Nostradamus predicted that he would die on 2 July 1566. Did he?
- Which four Smarties colours are also the names of characters in *Reservoir Dogs*?

11
Not Quite Playing the Game

'If you do not wish to be lied to, do not ask questions. If there were no questions, there would be no lies.'

(B Traven)

And then there's what we will call The Third Way.

Winning isn't everything, but it is an awful lot. If you cannot sweep to glorious victory by knowing everything, or by maximising your potential and cutting out unforced errors, then you really only have one option left: to cheat. In *EastEnders* Ian Beale catches three characters we haven't seen before whispering into a mobile phone halfway through the Queen Vic's weekly quiz. 'Oi!' he shouts. Albert Square's worthies flex their muscles, and within seconds the cheats are sent packing, swearing an undying revenge that everyone will have forgotten about by this time next week. As indeed they forgot about the pub quiz, which only served as a plot device in *EastEnders* for as long as someone was cheating in it.

Meanwhile in Ambridge, genial Bert Fry, farmhand and sometime cricket umpire, has been showing remarkable aptitude in The Bull's weekly quiz. He knows this, he knows that, he knows them all, and the reason he knows them all is because he has the same quiz book from which landlord Sid

Perks takes all his questions. Only when he hasn't had time to learn a particular chapter does genial Bert come a cropper. Finally unmasked, he is persuaded to make himself unavailable for subsequent quiz nights in pursuance of some other unrelated plotline.

So the message is clear. In the eyes of cynical media folk, with their perpetual runny noses and their strange packages arriving by motorcycle courier at all hours, most quizzers are cheats. If we're not, it's only because we haven't yet worked out how to cheat and get away with it. The average pub quiz is a sham. Honest endeavour has no chance against teams with encyclopaedias sewn into their overcoats, laptops with modems connected to mobile phones trawling the Internet, or photocopies of tonight's answers sitting on their thighs. Corruption is rife. The beer is watered down. You might as well go home and shoot yourself.

Having several friends who write for radio and TV, and having been to pub quizzes with most of them, I can confirm that this is pure paranoia. TV writers are unusually bitter and twisted people with whole bags of McCain oven chips on their shoulders. Misanthropic by nature, they develop an especial hatred for their own characters, whom they bully and manipulate with stark cruelty. A pub quiz environment, such as the one in which the writers themselves came seventh a week ago, is just an excuse to treat them particularly badly. The result is only too predictable.

Real life is less predictable and, thankfully, less eventful. There is cheating – of course there is – but it is rarely so blatant and never so apocalyptic in its consequences. Cheats, when identified, are not usually chased down the street by a pack of righteous quizzers. More often than not they just come back the following week and cheat again.

Now it's my turn to be cynical. I don't wish to imply any tacit approval of cheating, nor to suggest that other more scrupulous quiz participants should abandon their ways of rectitude and join in. For etiquette on this matter is clear. Cheating is unacceptable, and unaccepted by perhaps 98 per cent of quizzers. Most pub quizzes are, in fact, squeaky clean. Why wouldn't they be? If there were something at stake – something besides a good evening and a few quid at the end of it – you could begin to think of reasons to cheat. Whereas in an average pub quiz, most cheating is for the sake of cheating. Which almost seems worse.

Trouble is, identifying cheating is much easier than policing it. We had such a problem a few years ago in The Wrestlers, when Chris and Barry were still running the quiz. A new team had arrived, and each week, during the half-time recess, one of them would rise from his seat, walk the length of the bar and make a call from the payphone just inside the front door. Note the lack of subtlety in his method. This man made no attempt to conceal his underhand researching activities, or indeed the list of unanswered questions he propped next to the phone. Always dressed in the same grey suit, relaxing perhaps after a hard day at the office bullying minions and touching up his secretary, he would stand each week at the payphone, checking off the answers, utterly insensitive to the shocked stares coming from all directions.

What to do? The landlord, who couldn't have confronted a Cornish pasty, elected to do nothing. Chris and Barry didn't even notice: they were too busy at the time marking answer sheets, a task I have since come to realise can slow all brain activity to a crawl.

The rest of us, though, were enraged. How dare they? Unfortunately, as Terence was the first to point out, several of this man's team-mates were on the burly side of strapping. We feared for our health should we choose to make a stand, and all the other regular teams obviously felt the same. Cowardice is an unworthy emotion, unless it's your own, in which case it makes robust good sense. Instead of confrontation, then, our preferred tactic was to emanate silent hostility. Dark looks at the bar. Dark looks in the urinal. They probably thought we were trying to pick them up. As Neville Chamberlain discovered when he tried to emanate silent hostility at the Nazis, this is at best a short-term solution. The cheats carried on cheating just as before. After the second or third week a couple of us collared Chris and Barry before the evening's quiz and asked them to keep an eye out. Chris and Barry were relieved we had told them, or at least they said they were. (Much later, when I had come to know Chris better, I asked him how he had really felt. 'Brown trousers,' he admitted. He had noticed how big the man in the suit's friends were too.)

Nonetheless, the calls continued. Something had to be done. Then Richard hit upon an idea: get to the phone first. If someone else could make a call, the man in the grey suit wouldn't be able to. Barely had Chris read out the last question of the first round than Richard bounded from his chair and raced the length of the pub like an Olympic walker. He won by a short head, dropped a pound coin into the slot and enjoyed a long and, it has to be said, aimless conversation with his own answering machine. The man in the suit waited patiently. Then, less patiently. Finally, rather threateningly. As the deadline bell for handing in the answer sheets rang, Richard hung up. It was all we could do not to cheer.

A week later the man in the suit was ready for us. Richard thought he would make his move just as Chris was reading the last question, but with the sort of anticipation that makes footballers multi-millionaires, the man in the suit leaped up in the middle of the penultimate question. By now everyone in the pub had noticed. You could have cut the atmosphere with a knife and served it for tea.

The wild, yowling irony of all this was that the man in the suit's team never once won. They may have rung up for answers – we imagined some put-upon spouse sitting at the other end of the phone in candlelight, leafing through a heavy, out-of-date encyclopaedia – but obviously they never rang up for the right ones. Or perhaps the right ones they rang up for could never make up for the many wrong ones they had worked out for themselves. George thought they might have been an anarchist surrealist quiz team, dedicated to mischief and discord. Only when we looked at those huge blokes with their piggy eyes and protruding foreheads did we realise that they were probably just a bit thick.

In the end Chris, who is braver than he looks, had a word and the man in the suit and his friends disappeared from sight. For a few weeks afterwards we all left the pub remarkably cautiously, just in case hostile figures the size of double-decker buses were lurking in the shadows. But they never were. No doubt they took up some other pastime: needlepoint, perhaps, or far right-wing politics.

There are degrees of cheating, just as there are degrees of lying, of taking days off work, of rolling on the ground after being tackled from behind and of virtually every other activity Walt Disney wouldn't have approved of. On the lower slopes of moral turpitude, for instance, would come the Furtive Reference to Today's Newspaper. A question is asked that requires up-to-the-moment knowledge. You know that the relevant fact is in your paper, and you know that your paper is folded neatly in your lap. Only Disney, and possibly St Francis of Assisi, would not open the paper in a clandestine manner and check the answer for themselves. This isn't cheating so much as sensible use of resources, which is to say that of course it's cheating but virtually everyone does it from time to time. (In more conscientiously run quizzes than ours, and all quiz competitions, looking things up in papers is specifically outlawed, under which circumstances it immediately becomes a much graver offence. For more precise delineations of relative evil-doing, consult your local priest.)

A notch or two above opening a newspaper on the turpi-tude-ometer is the Furtive Reference to The Pocket Diary. It's not your fault that you happen to be carrying your pocket diary, even though you never carry it anywhere else. It is so neat and convenient, and contains many items of information that are of no conceivable interest or use to anyone who isn't taking part in a pub quiz. Dates of religious festivals? We got 'em. Stations on the London Underground? International Direct Dialling Codes? World Standard Time Zones? We got 'em all. The sheer ease of consulting this villainous little volume can blind you to the moral considerations, at which moment, if you were a cartoon character, a small angel version of you would appear over one shoulder and a small devil version of you over the other. 'Go on,' says Devil, smoking a cigar, 'take a look.' 'You'll be damned for ever,' says Angel, sententiously. It's up to you, of course, although if there were only a couple of points in it, I would be sorely tempted.

Any more substantial volume of reference, it goes without saying, is strictly not on. Furtive Reference to Encyclopaedia Hidden In Bushes Outside Pub is ingenious but unforgivable. And Furtive Reference to One of Those Nasty Little Books of Quiz Answers is liable to get you beaten up. In the Prince of Wales we eschew violence in all forms, for previously explained reasons of abject cowardice. But anyone spotted consulting such a volume may end up with a full pint of beer accidentally spilt over their trousers, a message that is impossible to disregard.

A more standard form of rule-bending is what has become broadly known as 'Earwigging'. Some teams have more acute hearing than others, and can tune into the deliberations of teams several tables away. Fortunately their body language usually lets them down. Anyone trying hard to listen to someone else cannot help but lean slightly in their direction and point their ears (often large, with flappy lobes and enough tufts of bristly hair sprouting from within to stuff a cushion) directly at the chosen sound source. There was one team in the Prince so notorious for earwigging that other teams thought twice before sitting even two tables away. If they arrived early, the Earwigs would try to cut out the middleman and sit on the table directly next to the quizmaster's, where earwigging could save many minutes of needless effort trying to work out what the answers were.

Which brings us to the related sin of 'Eyewigging'. Although there is no known insect called the eyewig, there might as well be if some of the teams we have played against had anything to do with it. Earwigs prowl around with their ears to the ground and everywhere else. Eyewigs never blink, and can read the tiniest handwriting upside down. Some brush past on the way to the loo and lean over accidentally on purpose for a swift look. Others just try to read your answer sheet from afar, as though staring through a telescope. One legendary team of Eyewigs included someone who was severely deaf. Everyone else naturally assumed that he wasn't really deaf at all, but merely listening in on other teams with his high-powered hearing aid. In fact he was just as deaf as he made out. What everyone failed to guess was that he was also an expert lip-reader. As Chris would say, 'Careless talk costs points.'

Eyewigging, not surprisingly, can generate severe paranoia and rampant hostility, leading to behaviour which may err on the wrong side of infantile. It becomes normal, for instance, to screen your answers when anyone from another team walks past, just as you would have screened your answers to questions 3 to 6 in the end-of-term maths test. People stare at one another suspiciously, each convinced that the other wants their answers. Then when you realise that the other bloke thinks you want his answers, you stare back in disgust that anyone should suspect you of such a thing. Meanwhile the real Eyewig has just edged past on his way to the bar and memorised your entire answer sheet.

Who can trust anyone else ever again? When you consider the enormity of earwigging and eyewigging, the foul simplicity of the mobile phone and the sheer braingrinding pointlessness of the quiz answer book, it's hard not to regard the whole of the human race with grave suspicion. As well as the bright, beautiful and gifted, pub quizzes also attract the socially inept and the socially inert: those men in the corner who never talk to anyone and believe aliens are among us. But were they always like this, or have years of quizzing paranoia eroded once trusting and outgoing personalities? Like the quizzer who wants to know everything, the quizzer who trusts no one can find himself on an already slippery slope recently greased with margarine. That way madness lies, and all other roads are closed. Far fewer people cheat than believe that everyone else is cheating – but try telling them that.

The worst, most embarrassing consequence of such paranoia is that you could end up accusing someone of cheating who wasn't cheating at all. Blush now, from head to toe, for all of us have harboured such suspicions at some time, and only the lucky few have never got round to doing anything about it. In the Prince of Wales we had a team who arrived apparently from nowhere and started to enjoy a spate of commanding victories. This wasn't suspicious in itself, although it was hugely annoying. George was especially put out: their condescending manner after each triumph might have been designed to provoke him and him alone. Paranoia now moved in for the kill. I noticed that one of the winning team always vanished to the loo between rounds. Off he would trot, his bladder palpably compromised by what appeared to be a dangerously high intake of Pepsi-Cola. But as George pointed out, he always made it back to his seat before his team-mates handed in their answer sheet. This team were becoming famous not just for winning but for handing in their answer sheets at the last possible moment. We watched them more closely. Toilet man would return and whisper to his team captain, who would hurriedly scrawl down some answers and hand them in.

Draw your own conclusions.

We certainly did.

The wrong ones.

But it's so easy to do. Consider the evidence. (1) This team kept winning – a suspicious activity in itself. (2) Toilet Man looked faintly untrustworthy. (3) No one needs to pee that often. Well, no one under sixty, anyway. (4) He never went for a pee after the quiz had finished, when everyone is usually bursting. (5) When George followed him into the Gents, he locked himself in the cubicle. All right, that's understandable behaviour when followed into the Gents by an irascible Scotsman, but even so. (6) George could hear no urinary splishing or sploshing, but he could hear the rustle of paper. (7) Not bog paper, normal paper. (8) Toilet Man always flushed the loo at the end, even though he hadn't used it. Or had he? (9) We were thoroughly confused.

As at The Wrestlers a year or two before, other teams started to notice. Toilet Man's regular trips to the Gents attracted more attention than a fair number of the questions: everyone shouted 'Read that again!' after he had walked by and distracted them from their task. People began to talk. Various theories were mooted.

- That he had an encyclopaedia or equivalent reference text
  concealed somewhere in the lavatory. (Rejected after
  Chris had a look in the cistern.)

- That he had in his pocket a small book of answers, which he consulted in the relative privacy of the cubicle. (Hard to prove, hard to disprove.)
- That he had a newspaper or similar publication secreted about his person. (Unlikely: too bulky.)
- That he was whispering into a mobile phone. (No evidence for this whatsoever, so it instantly became the favoured option.)
- That he had a distressing urinary infection which he attempted to conceal by rustling sheets of paper suspiciously. (All right, perhaps not.)

As at The Wrestlers, no one did anything, but we certainly discussed it enough. Teams who had never addressed a word to each other could now be found huddled together exchanging the latest theories. For the first time you could sense a genuine camaraderie between the regulars. Competitiveness and inherent diffidence had kept us apart. Now the chance that someone might be cheating was bringing us together. We were turning into a real little community. Or a lynch mob.

No one gave Toilet Man the benefit of the doubt. Despite an abject lack of hard evidence, we all jumped to the same conclusion. Once or twice Toilet Man varied his routine by nipping out through the back door for a walk in the square. Everyone assumed he was going to make a phone call. George followed him and hid behind a tree. But Toilet Man just walked about a bit, muttered to himself a little (was he wearing a headset? some other miniaturised communications device?) and wandered back into the pub. No proof, no evidence, no case to answer. He had to be up to no good.

Hilariously, though, his team's winning streak had abruptly ceased. Although his team-mates were still the last to hand in their answer sheets, having deliberated over their answers with agonising slowness, their luck and knowledge seemed to have deserted them. If they had been cheating, they were no longer doing it to much effect. But most of us, by now, were far beyond the reach of common sense. Loud, pointed comments were being made in the team's hearing. Tanja, our Dutch landlady, had been informed of the controversy, and had felt it necessary to announce before the quiz one week that cheating would not be tolerated – which completely bemused the team it was aimed at and several other occasional teams who hadn't a clue what was going on. Eventually, after an unusually drunken night of bitter mumblings, Chris and George went over for a chat. Terence and I feebly remained behind, saying nothing and wondering how it was all going to pan out. Terence sat by the door, presumably in case he had to make a quick getaway. I just felt sick, although some hastily consumed Prince of Wales sandwiches may have had something to do with that. We could hear Chris laughing, which he often does when embarrassed, although Terence fancied he could hear relief there as well. George said little and tried to look menacing. After ten minutes or so of intense conversation, the two of them wandered back to our table. 'Well?' I said, meaning 'Will I ever be able to set foot in this pub again?'

We had got it wrong. They were innocent. It hadn't even occurred to them that anyone might have suspected them. They were amazed. They were horrified. Toilet Man didn't go to the loo to consult anyone or anything. He just liked to collect his thoughts, look over his notes (written on rough paper), think things through. But cheat? Good Lord no.

Chris coughed a mortified cough. He was convinced we had made a terrible mistake. George was silent. He wasn't convinced of anything. Terence thought this would be a good time to leave. I agreed.

The next few weeks were almost surreally uncomfortable. Having done so much to stoke up this atmosphere of mutual distrust and recrimination, I felt obliged to repair the damage personally. I went around talking to people, explaining that I thought we had misjudged the Toilets (as they were becoming known) and pointing out their new-found Inability to Win. At the same time Toilet Man began to restrict his visits to the Gents, and was careful not to wear any item of clothing that might be thought by the suspicious (George) to conceal contraband reference books. That the Toilets continued to turn up at all we interpreted as proof of their innocence. The guilty would have drifted away eventually, unable to bear the burden of their terrible crime. But the Toilets came each week, still handed in their answer sheets after everyone else, and queried any question they thought was crap. They do all these things to this day, and no one (even George) doubts their integrity.

In short, we got away with it. Other teams in other pubs would have reacted less generously. (I told this story to a team we know from a darker and tougher pub than ours. They muttered something about having ears sewn back on.) But the Toilets' experience shows that it's dangerous not just to cheat, but to appear to cheat as well. And if you appear to cheat but do not cheat? Then you can find yourself in the shit right up to your neck, and so can everyone else.

Answers to Quiz 5

Goal shooter, goal attack, wing attack, centre, wing defence, goal defence and goalkeeper are the seven playing positions in netball. Colonel Paul W Tibbets was a decorated US bomber pilot in World War Two; his mother (after whom he named his plane, which dropped the bomb on Hiroshima) was called Enola Gay. Isla Nublar was the home of Jurassic Park. Nostradamus predicted that he would die on 2 July 1566 – and he did. The four Smarties colours that are also the names of characters in *Reservoir Dogs* are Mr Orange, Mr Blue, Mr Brown and Mr Pink.

Quiz 6

- Only one of the following actresses' names is her real name, as opposed to one made up by the Hollywood studio she was signed to: Rita Hayworth, Joan Crawford, Jean Harlow, Mae West, Lauren Bacall. Which one?
- In the Paris Olympiad of 1900 Leon de Lunden of Belgium won the gold medal in the only sport in Olympic history that involved the deliberate killing of animals. What was the discipline?
- One opera, one violin concerto, one ballet, seventeen string quartets, thirty-two piano sonatas. How many symphonies?
- Sweden did it in 1921. Britain did it in 1965. France did it in 1981. What?
- Which London theatre has the same name as a hard white metal with atomic number 46?

12
Tournament

*'Had we lived, I should have had a tale to tell of the
hardihood, endurance, and courage of my companions
which would have stirred the heart of every Englishman.
These rough notes and our dead bodies must tell the tale.'*

(Captain Robert Falcon Scott)

Sooner or later you will enter some sort of quiz tournament.
No, don't pull that face. Sooner or later you will enter some
sort of quiz tournament, whether you like it or not.

For the weekly pub quiz, though great fun, eventually
comes to lack the hard edge of brutal competition upon which
we all secretly thrive. Mountaineers tackle ever larger and
more fearsome peaks, and when they have ticked all the best
ones off the list they just tackle them again, only this time
without oxygen or tents or shoes. The poet, having mastered
the techniques of iambic pentameter, leaps without pause into
sonnet form, pausing only to knock off a few limericks during
his coffee break. New challenges are what keep the human
race going, and for a pub quizzer this usually means harder,
tougher pub quizzes. If you are going to be the best, you have
to play and beat the best.

Needless to say, it never works out like that. It is highly
unlikely that you will ever be the best, because someone else
with no life and an awful lot of reference books will always be
better. However clever you may be, there will always be a

question to which you do not know the answer. (On *Fifteen-To-One* it is often the first one you are asked.) Unanswerable questions are forever lying in wait, and the more competitive the quiz, the more eagerly they will pounce. In a hard-fought tournament it is not a matter of whether you will look a fool: it is a matter of when. Even if you sprint through the early rounds with barely a wrong answer, you are bound to crash into the Great Wall of Ignorance sooner or later. And that's assuming you are not tripped up by someone else first. Imagine the scene. You and your team stride into the quizzing arena, bursting with unjustified confidence. You fear no one. But there, nestling amongst your opponents like a puff adder, sits Kevin Ashman, larger than life and twice as clever. You might as well call for a cab right now. The best you will do tonight is lose, and even that may be a struggle.

Entering a pub quiz tournament is at best a waste of your time and at worst a drain on your very life force, emptying you like a giant syringe plunged at random into somewhere nasty. This may seem a rather grandiloquent way of describing a few Wednesday evenings spent in pubs even drabber and more run down than your own. But these contests are designed, as if by Nazi scientists, to get under your skin. Try as you might, you will never be able to take part in a half-hearted way, ambling along each week as though it does not really matter whether or not you qualify for the next round. You can feign such nonchalance, but no one will be fooled. What actually happens is that competitive instincts you never knew you had – or shamefully hoped you had grown out of – burst to the surface like a rash. And once you have started scratching this rash, it will never stop itching. Mmm, lovely and red now. Scratch scratch scratch.

Breweries know this, as do marketing departments of newspapers, publishers of reference books and indeed any organisation that wishes to attract some attention without any noticeable financial outlay. Announce a pub quiz tournament in the smallest display ad the eye can perceive, and droves of dedicated factheads will sign up, happy to sacrifice their peace of mind for an infinitesimal chance of glory. Certainly, we did. It's hard to remember now exactly how it came about. Perhaps one evening I had suggested that it might be fun to stretch ourselves further. (George remembers that I made some disingenuous comment about my need to research this book.) Whatever the case, Chris walked in the following week brandishing a newspaper clipping advertising the *Evening Standard* Pub Quiz Challenge. We grinned sheepishly at each other, as though contemplating a minor fraud, and filled in the form before we could change our minds. It was like one of those moments in a novel when the hero, presented with two contrasting options, heroically takes the wrong one, and the novelist, with a fiendish chortle, writes: 'He was to regret this decision for the rest of his life.'

The first problem was personnel. Half a dozen of us regularly turn up for the Prince of Wales quiz, and another three or four people with busier lives come from time to time. All were keen to take part in the *Evening Standard* competition, which required teams of precisely four. Who was to choose? Who was to be chosen? Obviously I had to be involved, as had Chris, who had signed the form, as had Terence, who is my oldest friend and knows a lot about football, as does George, who is small, Scottish and bald. To be fair we were the four who showed up most frequently on Tuesdays, and we were all willing to commit ourselves to several consecutive Wednesdays of nail-biting tension. But the others were miffed at being excluded. 'So I suppose he knows much more than I do?' said one. No, of course not, I lied. We could almost have been back in the school gymnasium, just as football teams or basketball teams or whatever were being selected from the available talent. Huge strapping boys had either already been picked, or were doing the picking, and enjoying it too much. Small weedy boys and lardy greedy boys did not care which team they played for, just as long as they weren't chosen last. Like the *Evening Standard* Pub Quiz Challenge, it didn't matter at all, and it mattered an awful lot.

My old comedy writing friend Michael, who had recently moved nearby, agreed to be our regular substitute, mainly because he could never have guaranteed to make every Wednesday evening anyway. Scarcely had we filled in the entry form, though, than we were contemplating the threat of round one, leg one. The contest, we discovered, was a straightforward knockout, with each round played over two legs, one at home and one away. There's something distinctly romantic about an away-leg in anything: venturing into hostile territory, trying to 'get a result', escaping with your life. Football is awash with tales of away-leg derring-do. Plucky British clubs drawn in the UEFA Cup against little known teams from northern Norway or darkest Latvia, losing their kit at one airport and their goalkeeper at another, while their fans roam the streets looking for bars in which to practise the only word of the local language they know ('beer'). Home advantage, in such circumstances, means more than a large and unruly crowd firing airguns at your back four. It represents the sheer bloodcurdling strangeness of your opponents: their ineradicable different-to-youness, not to mention their characteristic wad-of-notes-in-the-referee's-suitcaseness, against which there is no known defence. The chasm between two disparate cultures could hardly be emphasised more starkly. Or at least, such were our thoughts when we found out that we had been drawn in the first round against a pub in Finsbury Park.

The first leg, in fact, was at home. None of us could remember from our close reading of football match reports whether this was supposed to be an advantage or a disadvantage, although we knew for certain that it was one or the other. By now the basic rules of the quiz had been explained to us, and rapidly forgotten. There would be eight rounds of questions. Each round would consist of four pairs of questions. Each pair would be on the same subject, with team A answering the first question and team B answering the second. If team A got theirs wrong, team B could have a go for a bonus point, and vice versa. There was more of this, much more. We all half-listened, confident that someone else was doing the real listening. Then we heard the words 'individual round', and started listening properly.

'Individual, as in "by yourself"?' asked Terence, with a gulp.

'No, individual in the original, rarely used sense of the word, meaning "altogether in a big group, being waited upon by luscious handmaidens bearing trays of exotic sweetmeats",' said George, who can be a stickler for these things.

Chris, having taken part in many quiz competitions in a long and fact-filled life, nodded sagely. The dread words 'individual round' did mean what we thought they meant. Answering questions by ourselves. No conferring. All eyes on you. Mind blank. Trousers brown.

There would be two of these horrors lying in wait somewhere among the evening's eight rounds. For each individual round we would be given a list of the four subjects on offer, and would have to decide then and there which ones each of us was willing to handle. 'Etruscan pottery . . . Baroque opera . . . Keynesian macroeconomics . . . Rugby League . . . Who wants what?' Or, to put it another way, who wants to create a diversion while the rest of us run away?

The icing on the cake, though, was the mischievous imposition of a Joker on each of these individual rounds. Every other question in the quiz would be worth two points, but whoever was lumbered with the Joker would have to answer his question knowing that four points were at stake. If he got it wrong, the potential bonus to his counterpart on the other team was also doubled, to two points. So if you got an easy one wrong, you'd lose the four points you should have scored, while the other team gained two points when they got the answer right – which would mean six points lost, which could make all the difference in a close game. Which did make all the difference in a close game, as we later discovered.

First round, first leg, third pint of beer. I was ridiculously nervous. George had cried off at about lunchtime, for reasons I had been too angry to listen to properly. Some never-to-be-repeated opportunity to do something that no one else would want to do had come up, so George had tendered his most sincere apologies and assured me he would still be okay for the second leg the following week. I had therefore spent half the afternoon on the telephone trying to find a suitable substitute. The rules of the contest decreed that if you turned up with a team of only three you would sacrifice so many points that there wasn't any real point in turning up at all. This seemed outrageously unfair at first sight, although it's hard to see how else they could have arranged it. You had to ensure that all four members of each team were there on the dot of 8:30, and if one of them was stuck in a traffic jam or had been abducted by aliens, that was simply bad luck. This, however, is calm hindsight talking. At the time I had been cursing all Scotsmen in their mid-thirties. George's defection, though obviously feeble, could not be allowed to sabotage our entire campaign. It had taken me until late afternoon to track down Michael, who amazingly agreed to wriggle out of his previous commitment to help us out. At 8:15, then, Terence, Chris, Michael and I sat in the Prince of Wales, silently and suspiciously staring at our opponents, who, equally suspiciously and silently, stared back at us.

You never know who you are going to come up against in these competitions. All sorts of teams from all sorts of pubs enter, because most of them fill out the form after a few drinks, just as we had done. They could be a bunch of layabouts in it for the free sandwiches at half time. Or they could all be ex-*Mastermind* winners, their giant brains pickled in facts. It's the luck of the draw, as it is in the FA Cup or any other sporting knockout. But at least in the FA Cup you know roughly what sort of standard to expect. If you are drawn away to Manchester United, you don't turn up at Old Trafford on the day and think 'Oh, this is a big place, this side might be quite good.' In pub quiz tournaments, most oppositions look much the same. They will probably all be male. They will be losing their hair. At least two will be wearing thick glasses. George will say that one of them looks remarkably like a recent Grand Finalist on *Fifteen-To-One*. Another one will be wearing a very nasty waistcoat. They could know nothing. Or they could know *absolutely everything*.

Another slight problem, for more sensitive participants, is the manifest artificiality of the whole occasion. On a normal quiz night we all know why we are there, and anybody who does not want to be there leaves quickly. The *Evening Standard* Pub Quiz Challenge, by contrast, takes place on a normal non-quizzing night when normal non-quizzing people might have come in for a drink. How strange for them to see these two groups of men sitting nervously at adjacent tables, fingering piles of scrap paper, slurping up lager at an unhealthy rate, and wondering where to hide the large slabs of printed cardboard that announce that they are representing their pubs in the *Evening Standard* Pub Quiz Challenge. You feel like a dork, because, viewed dispassionately, that is what you are.

Our first round opponents from Finsbury Park looked ominously clever, which is to say they looked like perfectly normal people that you would see in a pub anywhere. Psyching yourself out before a single question has been asked is not the ideal strategy, but it's easily done. We won the toss and elected to be team B for the first four rounds. Chris had heard somewhere that it was an advantage to be team B first; later the opposition told us that they had heard somewhere that it was an advantage to be team A. For our first question we were asked to name the Russian spacecraft that had recently been servicing the perennially crumbling space station Mir. We looked at each other, stunned into silence. 'Was it one of the Salyuts?' someone said. 'No, can't be,' someone else said. 'I'm sure it's not,' I said. 'We don't know,' I said to the Prince of Wales's landlady Tanja, who was acting as questionmaster. The answer was Salyut. 'Oh for Christ's sake,' said Chris. He had a point.

Slowly we relaxed and began to concentrate, and even get a few questions right. Adrenalin began to flow. 'Yessss!' I shouted after we had pulled a correct answer out of the air. At least twice we all felt a strange yearning to exchange high fives. Only the pub's impossibly polite atmosphere stopped us. When the first individual round came up we were two points ahead. One of the four subjects was 'Movie Stars', which sounded relatively straightforward. As the endorphins roared through my brain, I volunteered to take it on, with the Joker.

How hard could a question on Movie Stars be? Chris had warned us to take nothing for granted. The company that had set the questions, Burns & Porter, are well known for their sometimes random definitions of what might be considered 'general knowledge'. But I was confident. I knew who had played Vito Corleone's sons in *The Godfather*.[1] I knew the name of Olivia de Havilland's movie star sister.[2] How hard could it be?

---

[1] Al Pacino, James Caan, John Cazale.
[2] Joan Fontaine.

You couldn't fault Tanja. She never let on. 'Marcus, playing the joker on "Movie Stars". For four points then. Which movie star's name . . .' Pause for breath. (Yes? Yes?) 'Which movie star's name . . . is an anagram of "stricken ovens"?'

What?

Tanja stared at me for a second. 'Which movie star's name is an anagram of "stricken ovens"?' I had heard her the first time, but I hadn't realised that I had shouted 'What?' rather than merely thinking it. Chris knew the answer, of course. He completes *The Times* crossword between Underground stations and had known before I did that my name is an anagram of 'Mark Bumscanner'. Each of us has his quizzing talents: anagrams are not mine. I had no idea what the answer was. My mind was as blank as a zen master's. I had thirty seconds in which to answer; how long it took those thirty seconds to pass I could not tell you. 'Stricken ovens'? All I could see in my mind's eye was a very sad gas cooker. Was that the sound of the cooker crying, or was it me?

Luckily the other team did not know the answer either. 'Kevin Costner!' said Tanja. I was incensed. What sort of stupid question was that? Meanwhile my oppo on the other team was grappling with his own anagram, 'big melons'. He worked it out after twenty seconds, trying not to be distracted by the steam now whooshing out of my ears. 'Mel Gibson!' he announced with a grin. Two points.

In any quiz you place yourself within the power of the people who set the questions. In a quiz tournament, when the stakes are so much higher, you are at their mercy. In the second individual round one of the subjects was Natural History. Michael has a degree in biology and a knowledge of small furry animals that would put David Attenborough to shame. Obvious Joker material, in short, which meant he never had a chance. 'What sort of animal is a jacana?' asked Tanja. Michael's mouth fell open. When asked to identify an animal you have never heard of, the best bet is to say either 'fish' or 'bird', which may be why Michael said, 'Is it a type of cat?' It was a bird.

And yet in the same round the subject we were all most determined to avoid was Theatre. The finer points of restoration comedy perhaps, or a small thesis on absurdist drama: we feared the worst, and so gave the question to Terence, who said he was happy to undertake the burden on the strict understanding that we should not expect him to get it right. Perfectly reasonable: we were all too delighted to avoid the category ourselves to start quibbling. And the question? 'What is the name of the area in the theatre where the audience sits?' Terence's mouth also fell open. Had we been sea mammals coursing through the ocean, we would have ingested a lot of plankton between us that evening. Obviously, this being an individual round, we could not assist him in any way (hastily scribbled notes on pieces of scrap paper being especially frowned upon). All we could do was observe his reactions, which in the space of about three seconds proceeded as follows:

1 Answer. I know the answer.
2 Question. The only reason I know the answer is because it is an incredibly easy question.
3 Disbelief. Mind shuts down for several micro-seconds.
4 Suspicion. Surely it cannot be that easy. Maybe it's a trick question.
5 Confusion. Inability to think of any other explanation. It's just a very easy question.
6 Conscious again. Time to say something.
7 Mouth says 'Auditorium' with slightly quizzical tone in voice just in case this is all a horrible trick after all and I am going to look very foolish. Still can't quite believe it when tucking into half-time sandwiches a few minutes later.

You can't blame him, though. If you were answering a question about motoring you would not necessarily expect to be asked what they call those four round things you find at each corner of a car. But Chris had warned us. Burns & Porter's reputation precedes them. As one old quizzer later told me, you never get used to it. You think they have asked the stupidest question anyone could possibly ask, and then they ask one stupider. It always takes you by surprise.

Nonetheless, by this stage we were beginning to open up a lead. Following the absent George's example I had become convinced that the quietest member of their team, who called himself 'Dermot', was in reality a Dubliner called John who had been in at least two *Fifteen-To-One* Grand Finals and had a mind like a meat cleaver. But after 'Dermot' contributed a couple of routine wrong answers, and I had calmed myself down with more lager, I realised that 'Dermot' was not John at all, but Dermot. He was human, I was a bit drunk and by the end of eight exhausting rounds we were 12 points ahead.

We sat back, and exhaled in unison. Vast amounts of sighing and exhaling seem to follow the last question of a quiz, as though no one has found time to breathe efficiently for several hours. You expect to feel triumph, and so does all the adrenalin splashing around in the nervous system. But this was just the first leg, the home leg. If we had been playing football, we would expect to be a goal or two up at this stage. Next Wednesday we would venture into our opponents' territory, an unknown hostile environment far beyond Crouch End and deep in the alien postcode known as 'N5'. Rough area, we agreed. Anything could happen. 'Be especially careful of prawn sandwiches,' said Chris, the voice of experience.

So as we wandered out into North London's scarcely breathable night air, we were full of relief and alcohol in about equal measures. After serious quiz duties had been completed, the competition's rules had given us the opportunity to play a 'just for fun' beer round of twenty questions. It was clear that neither team had felt like playing, but each had agreed out of politeness. At stake were the four pints of beer neither team would want to drink, as we had all had quite enough already and, after all those sandwiches, were beginning to feel a bit sick. Imagine if, at the end of a gruelling FA Cup tie, the referee asked the teams if they fancied playing half an hour's extra time 'just for fun'. Being British, though, we went through the motions, and after the proffered drinks had been graciously refused, we called it a night. A 12-point lead was as much as we could have hoped for. But quizzing is a game of two halves, and we would need 110 per cent on the away leg – possibly even 115 per cent, depending on the prawn sandwiches. I had indigestion just thinking about it.

Terence had already indicated that he was unavailable for the second leg the following Wednesday, so I quickly secured Michael's services. It seemed a strong line-up, with that sort of good-on-paper quality that can so easily squander a 12-point lead. Then disaster struck. George discovered that he would be spending Wednesday and Thursday at a residential course in High Wycombe. As we were battling our fearsome rivals from N5, he would be brushing up on the finer points of local government accounting. This displeased George intensely. (It did not do much for my mood either.) He was quite willing to miss the quiz for a hip party for which he had blagged an invitation on false pretences, but for work? In High Wycombe?

Chris, wise and calm as ever, had an idea. He was working in Luton that day. He could drive round the M25 to High Wycombe, pick up George, zip in on the M40, round the North Circular, and they could be in Finsbury Park before you could say Chicken McNuggets. 'Are you sure?' I said. 'No problem,' said Chris. 'We'll meet you there.'

The human race divides neatly into those who, upon hearing the words 'We'll meet you there', assume everything will work out as planned, and those who become completely convinced that calamity is just around the corner, followed closely by a plague of frogs. There is no need to explain which of the two groups Chris and I fall into; let it be enough merely to observe that at 8:15 the following Wednesday, in a pub somewhere in Finsbury Park, I had bitten my nails so brutally that my fingers were beginning to bleed. Two chairs at our table were unoccupied. Michael and I had only just arrived, ferried over by a minicab driver who had flown in from Ghana the previous day, and knew nothing of this 'Finsbury Park'. If we had had trouble finding the place, which was more artfully concealed within the backstreets of N5 than we had anticipated, then Chris and George, on their epic journey from Luton via High Wycombe, would be struggling to arrive before the weekend. And at 8:30, if they were not here, points would be lost, and probably the match with it.

Of course it is up to the opposition to decide how strictly these rules are to be adhered to. The home team, looking relaxed and magnanimous, seemed as amiable as they had the previous week. But how can you tell? As Chris had said, some of the teams you will encounter in a competition like this will be genuinely pleasant and good fun. Others will be complete bastards. Even they may not know which sort of team they are until the crunch comes.

8:22. The ticks of the pub clock were deafening. You would do well to hear Concorde take off if this clock were anywhere near. In between the ticks, the silence was no less deafening. 'Chris's mobile!' I shouted, leaping out of my chair. 'I could ring home, get the number, ask my girlfriend to call him, she could ask him where he was, ring back, tell us, then we'd know!' 'And that will enable him to get here that much more quickly, will it?' said Michael, wearily.

8:27. I still hadn't seen Dermot smile. Even now, as the seconds roared by, he was utterly impassive. What thoughts were passing through his mind? Michael and I were chatting to the landlady, in an attempt to keep the atmosphere light. Perhaps if we kept chatting, we could distract their attention until it was past 8:30. Perhaps I could pass out, or Michael could pretend to choke on a crisp. I wouldn't mind being beaten by a better team: actually, I would, immensely. But to be beaten by the M25? Surely life could not be so cruel.

8:29. *Tick. Tick. Tick. Tick.* Dermot looked up at the clock; a half-smile flitted across his lips. Oh fuck, I thought, we're in trouble. At that precise moment two bald men, one tall and bearded, the other short and wearing black, almost fell through the front door. 'I hope we're not late,' said Chris with a smile. 'Ah, it wouldn't have mattered if you had been,' said the home team's captain. 'We're not sticklers for that sort of thing here.'

In fact we won fairly easily that evening, but you don't want to hear about that now.

Answers to Quiz 6

Rita Hayworth was born Margarita Carmen Cansino, Joan Crawford was born Lucille Le Sueur, Jean Harlow was born Harlean Carpentier, Lauren Bacall was born Betty Joan Perske; Mae West was born Mae West. In the Paris Olympiad of 1900 Leon de Lunden of Belgium won a gold medal for live pigeon shooting. Beethoven composed one opera, one violin concerto, one ballet, seventeen string quartets, thirty-two piano sonatas – and nine symphonies. Sweden in 1921, Britain in 1965, France in 1981 all abolished the death penalty. The London theatre that has the same name as a hard white metal (atomic number 46) is the Palladium.

Quiz 7

- Cinema. Who played a brain surgeon in *Days of Thunder* and a nuclear physicist in *The Peacemaker*?
- Why should every philosophy student know the Danish word for churchyard?
- From the time of Edward the Confessor to Queen Anne, what was popularly believed to be the cure for the glandular disease scrofula?
- Which instrument of the modern orchestra can play the lowest note?
- What is the only country in the world whose name in English begins with the letter O? (For a bonus point, name a European country whose name begins with O in its own language.)

13
Good Quiz, Bad Quiz

*'What is the longest American state name you can spell
out using only the second line of a typewriter?'*
(Anonymous quizmaster)

'Groan.'
(Everyone else in pub)

Some quizzers are born pernickety. Others are made pernickety. A rare few have pernicketiness thrust upon them. Virtually all would now ask whether 'pernicketiness' is really the noun of 'pernickety'. It's just part of the territory.

'Take the Flake advert,' says George. ' "Only the crumbliest, flakiest chocolate tastes like chocolate never tasted before." They've been saying that for over thirty years. In that time virtually everyone in the British Isles has eaten a Flake at some time or other. And the basic formula of the bar hasn't changed since . . . when was it?'

'1911,' I say, having just asked a question to this end in the quiz.

'Right. So the last thing you could say for "the crumbliest, flakiest chocolate", the very last thing in the world, is that it "tastes like chocolate never tasted before". So what's that all about, then?'

Place pernickety people in a pub and they will argue about anything. Seating arrangements, lavatorial stench, the price of peanuts: it's all fair game, and the quiz is doubly so. Our moans about the Burns & Porter questions in the *Evening Standard* competition may have seemed unduly graceless, but they only echoed the moans of everyone who takes part in pub quizzes. Complaining about the questions is what we do – unless of course we have won, in which case the questions are among the most enlightened and ingenious quiz questions ever written.

Several years ago, some time before we showed up, the Prince of Wales started to buy in its quizzes from an outside supplier. A lot of pubs do this: it's cheap and it's easy, and at least you know the answers are likely to be right. The regulars were all for it. Until this point the onus of providing a quiz had fallen on the landlord, and some landlords had been better at it than others. Without traducing the landlord of the time, it is fair to say that everyone was bored of constantly being asked which film star was christened Maurice Micklewhite.[1]

So quizzes were purchased, and for a while peace and harmony reigned in London N6. It could never last. As the regulars soon realised, bought-in quizzes tend to lack a certain flavour. Produced in bulk and at speed by poorly remunerated quiz slaves, they rarely spring surprises, and the ones they do spring are not usually worth springing. They are the quizzing equivalent of tinned food – reliable but dull on the palate. Fresh quizzes may be more unpredictable, but at least they taste of something, and they are chock full of vitamins and fibre.

Once again the regulars grew restless. Didn't we have that one about the currency of Libya a couple of weeks ago? (Or was it Tunisia?) After lengthy and passionate debate it was

---

[1] Michael Caine.

agreed that this was not all a quiz could be. The questions were not up to scratch. In fact they were crap.

'So write your own,' said the landlord, rattled.

Hmm, thought the regulars. Maybe we can.

Ever since, teams have taken it in turns to set and deliver the Prince of Wales quiz. Each Tuesday a different face sits behind the microphone, sipping complimentary beers between questions and becoming less coherent as the evening wears on. As new teams arrive and settle into the weekly ritual, they decide that they too would like to have a go at setting questions and sipping complimentary beers. From time to time our landlady Tanja clumps upstairs to fetch her legendary diary (occasionally thrown out by mistake or lost down the side of a sofa for several weeks), and teams grab the first available dates. Many non-regulars assume that some arcane form of rota system is involved, but actually it is just first come first served. Bag a date before anyone else bags it, and a month or two later, when you stroll in just before nine on Tuesday, the quizmaster's table, the microphone, the score sheets and the pint jug full of coins will be set up for you. God help you should it have slipped your mind.

Setting quizzes is a natural progression from taking part in them. Just as entering bigger and sillier tournaments keeps the competitive muscles flexing, so the ability to write and deliver your own questions stops you moaning at the inadequacies of everybody else's. Perhaps surprisingly, most quizzers think long and hard before accepting this responsibility. Being British, we feign modesty and push ourselves forward only with the greatest reluctance. 'No, no, no,' we say disingenuously, 'surely it's someone else's turn.' We would rather lop off limbs than appear presumptuous. It's all nonsense, of course. The quizmaster's seat is the best in the house. Reluctant though we may be to take it, soon we shall be just as reluctant to vacate it. I had been a regular at the

Prince for over a year before I signed up to set my first quiz. I managed to wait a week before I signed up for my second. Even heroin doesn't work that quickly. The day after your first quiz, you mope about the house, pale and sweating. This gaping void at the core of your being: where has it come from? It wasn't there yesterday. It makes no sense. You try to keep yourself occupied. Read the paper, perhaps, or watch TV. As you do so, some silly little fact comes into your purview.

'Boudoir comes from the French word *bouder*, meaning to sulk.'

Sorry, did someone say something?

'California spends more on building and maintaining prisons than it does on higher education.'

And with a crack of intellectual lightning, your mind responds with the sentence that most quizzers come to recognise as their life sentence:

'Now that's a good quiz question.'

Repeat it to yourself. Feel how seductive it sounds.

'Now that's a good quiz question.'

Beautiful, isn't it? You can be doing anything – eating, reading, driving, talking, staring out of the window with saliva dribbling down your chin. A fact makes itself known to you. It is a good fact. You know how to make it a better fact. The neurons connect. A quiz question is created.

'It's a blessing and a curse,' said Russell the other day. 'Only without the blessing bit.' This is a fairly gloomy way of looking at things, although Russell's ways often are. But I can see what he means. Sometimes you would like to take in a piece of information without wondering how well it would fit into round three. It's as though some tiny alien quiz being has tunnelled into your cerebral cortex and is now controlling your mind. It isn't you who has volunteered to set the quiz this week. It isn't you who sits behind the microphone reading out questions in your Local Radio DJ voice. It isn't you who deflects challenges from teams who are convinced that most of your answers are wrong. Blame the tiny alien quiz being.

What you don't immediately realise is that compiling quizzes is only really the means to an end. Being quizmaster: that's where the serious fun lies. I once heard someone say that quizmastership was better than sex. 'Which shows how much sex he's having,' said George, not unreasonably. But if you are going to make the most of your stint as quizmaster – which effectively means being allowed to do it again at the earliest opportunity – you will have to come up with some decent questions. Quizzers can be a tough audience to please. They have heard them all before. They need to be cajoled, diverted, amused, bemused, indulged, tickled and finally dumbfounded by their own brilliance/idiocy. 'Why didn't we get that?' Not: 'How the fuck are we supposed to know that?' The difference between a good quiz and a bad quiz can be infinitesimal.

So what is the secret of setting a good quiz? For fear of sounding like Geoffrey Boycott ('Don't set your sights too high'), I would have to say that in the end there is no substitute for hard work, imagination, some well-developed critical faculties, a pile of up-to-date reference books and several episodes of *Fifteen-To-One* on tape. It takes a while to compile a decent quiz, and there's no way around it.

Even so, this is supposed to be fun, both for you and for the happy campers who will have to answer your questions. It's a matter of personal taste, but as far as I am concerned, the most memorable questions are the ones that sound hard and are in fact very easy indeed. For example:

Where in London would you find a Scottish fishing village, an Eastern European country, a South American river and a city in central Russia?

Well, fuck knows, as George would say. (This was from Joey and Carmel's Christmas quiz of 1996, a legendary night few of us remember clearly.) We sat and thought and brooded for five minutes or more, until someone mentioned the river Orinoco in Venezuela. In unison we all cried, 'The Wombles!' Scottish fishing village: Tobermory. Eastern European country: Great Uncle Bulgaria. City in central Russia: Tomsk. Answer: Wimbledon Common.

Or there was this one Russell once used (borrowed, I understand, from a 15th-century theologian):

Who in the Bible killed a quarter of the world's population?

You try and list some mass murderers of ancient times. Herod, perhaps? Some unforgettably villainous Pharaoh you have temporarily forgotten? You can waste a long time travelling down this cul de sac without realising how easy the answer is.[2] It's only the question that's difficult.

Cryptic conundrums like these are too fussy for some people, but there are always ways to twist dull facts into more interesting shapes. Since Mozambique joined the Commonwealth, for example, we have often been asked which member of the Commonwealth was never a constituent part of the British Empire. Either you know it or you don't know it, and if you do know it you are bored with it because you have been asked it 14,869 times before. So twist it a little:

Which is the only Commonwealth country to have Portuguese as its official language?

---

[2] Cain. Killed Abel. Doh!

It has to be Mozambique, once you think about it. But at least you would have to think about it, and perhaps argue a little as well. Which is all that is required.

There are no real rules about any of this, but you should bear certain things in mind. Accessibility: does the question fall within reasonable bounds of people's knowledge? Comprehensibility: does it make sense? Variety: have there been too many questions about 1960s' pop music for one week (or lifetime)? Humility: are you there to help people score points, or to score points off them? And perhaps most important of all, Gettability: is anyone going to get this right? If not, why ask it at all?

One area of controversy is the numerical question. Delicious though it may be to ask questions which require precise numerical answers, they must be used sparingly and with care. For instance, it's fine to ask in which centuries the Hundred Years' War was fought,[3] as there is only a limited number of possible answers. But it's not really on to ask how many days there are in a year on the planet Pluto[4] and expect anyone to get it right. Even if you gave a point for teams who were within, say, 10 per cent of the right answer, people would think, well, so what? In the ordinary run of things, numerical questions should either be incredibly easy –

Treasure Island. *In the pirates' song 'Yo ho ho and a bottle of rum' – how many men were on the dead man's chest?*[5]

– or sufficiently eccentric that your audience can at least guess the right answer:

---

[3] The 14th and 15th. Or, if you prefer, the 1300s and 1400s.
[4] 90,465.
[5] 15.

In the early 1800s, the whole of Europe's potato output could still be traced back to the first plants brought back by the Spanish from the New World. How many individual potato plants did the Spanish bring back?[6]

The exception to this is that most beloved of all pub quiz features, the tie-breaker. (My question about Cadbury's Flake was one such.) Circumstance will dictate that, from time to time, two or more teams will win with the same number of points. There has to be some way of dividing them, and an egregiously hard numerical question usually does the trick.

According to the Independent,[7] *it takes a man an average of 38 seconds to urinate. How long does it take a woman?*[8]

Whichever team is closest to the answer wins the prize. At the Prince of Wales this was so popular that a numerical tie-breaker was written into the bonus round. Teams answer five normal questions and the tie-breaker, because there is only one £10 drinks voucher to give away. Quizsetters vie with each other to dream up more annoying tie-breakers, freed at last of the need to please their audience.

As the crow flies, how many miles apart are Land's End and John O' Groats?[9]

---

[6] Two. This lack of genetic diversity is believed to have caused the Irish potato famine of 1845–9.
[7] Note this wonderfully pompous justification for the use of some unprovable factoid you spotted in yesterday's newspaper.
[8] 54 seconds. Go on, time yourself.
[9] 603.

In a 24-hour period, how many ewes can a ram service?[10]

Television. How many episodes were there of Crossroads?[11]

My all-time favourite was another of the many I liberated from *Fifteen-To-One.*

In which year in the future was H G Wells's story The Time Machine *set?*

It has to be a guess: you don't think you would remember it if you had been told, and if you had ever read the book, it was probably many years ago. Most teams put something like 2057 or 2123 or 2275. One team boldly plumped for 2587. They won, of course. The year in which *The Time Machine* was set was AD 802,701.

Good questions bring smiles to faces, or make people bang their heads against walls because they really should have got it. Bad questions, by contrast, merely induce a dull ache of despair. There is nothing anyone can do about a bad question. The power, as ever, lies in the hands of the quizmaster, and to some extent everyone trusts him not to abuse it. Of course bad questions will always slip though. Sometimes you don't know it's a stinker until you read it out and hear mystified grunts from all around you. But a whole string of bad questions plants a seed in the minds of those taking part, a seed that says, 'I'd rather be doing something else.' Rotten quizzes put people off, which is one reason that our quality control has become so stringent at the Prince of Wales. The other reason is that we're all difficult bastards.

---

[10] 40. Unless you know better . . .
[11] 4,510.

Bad questions devolve into three basic types, the Dull, the Stupid and the Wrong. The Dull are self-explanatory: the questions you have heard thousands of times before, and probably still don't know the answers to. Dull quiz shows, like Channel 5's excruciating *100 Per Cent*, specialise in such questions. Argentina is the world's eighth largest country: true or false? In fact it's true, but so what? In which year did Richard Attenborough receive his peerage, 1991, 1992 or 1993?[12] Even the most fascinating question can become dull with repetition, so imagine how dull an already dull question can become. Actually, don't imagine it: it's too dull a thought even to contemplate.

Stupid questions usually only exist to show everyone how clever the quizmaster is. No one will know the answer, and no one will want to have known it when the quizmaster finally reads it out. A stupid question, then, discriminates against everyone equally, but particularly against the quizmaster, who may not be asked again. One memorable tosser in the Prince of Wales asked the following:

> *'Marie Stopes was a famous biologist and birth control pioneer who died in 1958. What was the title of her only play?'*

Er, come again? Perhaps he should have gone the whole hog and asked us which brand of cigarettes she smoked. Everyone in the pub groaned. The quizmaster was delighted. No one would get this one, you could see him thinking, as thrilled with himself as he could be without bursting into flames. The answer, of course, was *Our Ostriches* (1923). What an arsehole. We saw him off too.

(In fact, as Chris pointed out, there's not a bad question hiding in there somewhere. *'Our Ostriches*, which was published

---

[12] In fact it was 1993, but does anyone (even Lord Attenborough) care?

in 1923, was the only play of which famous biologist and birth control pioneer?' It's not hard if you have heard of Marie Stopes, but at least you would have a chat and a laugh about it before writing down the right answer. Incidentally, Marie Stopes did not like the idea of getting old, so she only ever celebrated her twenty-sixth birthday. On her seventieth birthday, when she turned twenty-sixth for the forty-fifth time, she demonstrated her fitness and agility by sticking her big toe in her mouth.

A Wrong question can be the most galling of all. At one quiz, not unconnected with the publishing company whose name adorns this book, the quizmaster asked how frogs breathe. 'Through their skins,' thought several teams, and wrote this down. All were marked wrong. The quizmaster couldn't read his own writing, and was convinced that the correct answer was 'through their shins'. No one could persuade him that he had made a mistake, even though the likelihood of any animal inhaling and exhaling through bones in its lower limbs was not great. Amputee frogs would immediately suffocate, while anyone eating frogs' legs would be inadvertently consuming lungs. But no argument would sway him.

It's all about loss of face. I used to set my quizzes at the Prince of Wales with David, the one who has since moved to Oxfordshire but still drives down every few weeks and drinks diet Coke all evening. He's a staunch friend and no fool, but his grasp of the concept of factual accuracy can be slender. Whenever he stole questions from the Internet, which he did frequently, it was on the brave assumption that they were right. One day he asked the following:

'The number 34 shirt of the Chicago Bears was retired out of respect for which player?'

American football is not my subject, so I hadn't bothered to check the answer either. David thought it was O J Simpson;

everyone else in the pub, and several people waiting at the bus stop outside, knew it was Walter Payton. When David read the 'answer' out, there was uproar. 'No fucking way!' shouted George, who was sitting with Chris and Terence a few tables away. We had cocked up badly. David, though, is a proud man. He regards compromise as a sign of weakness, and won't countenance any action that might cause him to lose face. I thought we were more likely to lose face by insisting that our answer was the correct one, but he insisted that it stood. No one got the points. They had all written the wrong right answer instead of the right wrong answer. A mood of seething indignation swept through the pub like a bad cold. Perhaps it's unfair, but a quiz with 44 superb questions and one brainless one will always be remembered for the brainless one. As ever I was loyal and steadfast. 'It was his question,' I told everyone. 'I had nothing to do with it.'

Delivering a quiz is, of course, a skill in itself. It's strange, then, most quizmasters don't think it's a skill they need acquire. Nature, they believe, has already equipped them for this most burdensome of tasks. That ready wit, that effortless turn of phrase . . . three pints of cooking lager, and most of us think we have it taped. Whereas if we did have it taped, on a tape recorder for instance, we might hear how rambling, self-indulgent and incoherent we are.

The quizmaster who thinks he is funny is a tragic beast. The Minotaur was merely half man, half bull – hairier than he might have expected to be, and less likely to look cool in tight trousers. But at least he wasn't a quizmaster who thinks he is funny. The symbolic exhalation after each 'joke'. The droll 'quip' after each question. The inverted commas fall over each other to impose levels of irony our gag-laden quizmaster will never be able to understand.

Beer has much to do with it. Beer enhances confidence

while reducing performance. We know this. But beer also enhances confidence that performance is enhanced, while reducing everyone else's confidence in your ability to walk in a straight line and count up to six. An element of Dutch courage is useful, even advisable, before any performance. But in between questions you will gulp down that Dutch courage like a particularly thirsty cactus, so that by round three you will be a drivelling baboon, incapable of thought or action, and nurturing the sort of hangover that could cost you your livelihood.

The first time I delivered a quiz, I drank so much that I was flat out for two days afterwards. I don't know what came over me. High spirits? Adrenalin? Blind terror? A combination of the three seems the likeliest explanation. But that evening, once I drank through my fear, I had a whale of a time. For the following forty-eight hours I transformed myself into that whale, beached on various well-sprung surfaces in my flat and occasionally flapping my fins to attract my girlfriend's attention. It was a pitiful display. Fortunately we had only been going out for a short time, so she was easily convinced that this was some sort of one-off aberration. I tried to convince her that the next time was a one-off aberration as well, and the next time too – but by then the law of diminishing returns was beginning to wreak its usual havoc. These days I am a model of sobriety when I present the quiz – in that I eat a huge meal before I set out, and drink a single Coke at some point during the beerfest as a gesture towards moderation. This usually cuts down whale time to a more manageable twenty-four hours.

All quizmasters have their little habits, the phrases they cannot do without. William G Stewart says 'On we go' between questions, and even records a couple of extra 'On we go's' for the sound engineer to dub on to any awkward gap. Chris is incapable of just reading out the first question. He always has to say 'without further ado' to signpost it, a phrase

I have never heard him use under any other circumstances. (For some reason I am reminded of a newsagent near school who completed every single transaction with the litany 'Thanking you, much obliged, ta.')

My own worst habit is the tendency to preface every question with a one-word description of the subject it falls under. This too is stolen from *Fifteen-To-One*, where it's only appropriate, as contestants have three seconds to answer each question and so need to know exactly what they are being required to think about. 'Television. How many episodes were there of *Crossroads*?' is clear and precise, and if you didn't say 'Television' at the beginning, no one would know what you were talking about until you reached the word 'Crossroads', at which point the shock for some contestants might simply be too great.

In the Prince of Wales, though, it just sounds pompous. 'Are you sure you don't mean "authoritative"?' I asked Russell when he first told me this. 'No, no,' he replied, '"pompous" is definitely the word.' No one else had ever mentioned it before, although I had been wondering why my girlfriend, on her occasional visits to the quiz, had taken to holding her head in her hands. It just shows how difficult it is to strike the right balance. If you're not pompous, you're banal and chatty. If you're not drunk, you're terrified. If you're not sober, you're just an embarrassment. And that's even if all your questions are inspired and all your answers are right. Who'd be a quizmaster? Most of us, as often as we can.

Answers to Quiz 7

Nicole Kidman played a brain surgeon in *Days of Thunder* and a nuclear physicist in *The Peacemaker*. Every philosophy student may (or may not) know that the Danish for churchyard is

Kierkegaard. From the time of Edward the Confessor to
Queen Anne (clue) it was believed that the royal touch could
cure scrofula. The instrument in the modern orchestra that can
play the lowest note is the piano. The only country in the
world whose name in English begins with the letter O is
Oman. (The European country whose name begins with O in
its own language is Österreich, otherwise known as Austria.)

Quiz 8

• In August 1994, on a salvage mission to the seabed around
  the wreck of the *Titanic*, an item was discovered yards
  away from the liner's bridge, which, had it been used,
  might have saved the lives of 1,523 people on board. What
  item?
• Leofric, Earl of Mercia, died in 1057. How was his wife
  better known?
• Who came fourth in the Eurovision Song Contest in 1970
  singing a song called 'Gwendolyne'?
• What is the longest river that is wholly in England?
• Paul Gascoigne, when asked on live Norwegian TV
  before a Norway-England World Cup qualifier if he had a
  message for the Norwegian people, responded with which
  three words?

14
The Last 128

Winning is everything.
The only ones who remember you
when you come second are your wife
and your dog.

(Damon Hill)

We had won our first-round match in the *Evening Standard* Pub
Quiz Challenge, and were through to the last 128. What wondrous, magical words these were, although as Terence pointed
out, they were only half as wondrous and magical as 'the last
64'. As we celebrated our victory, our first thoughts were for
the 128 teams who had been knocked out in the first round.
'Ha ha ha ha ha ha!' we thought, 'we're through and you're
not!' As ever, Chris was on hand to douse our triumphalism.
Only he had found time to read the rules of the competition,
which stated that all the teams knocked out in round one
would now go through to a 'plate' competition, the winners of
which would be invited to rejoin the competition proper at a
later stage. In theory you could lose your first match and still
end up in the final. If you won your first match and lost your
second match, though, you would be eliminated.

In effect, then, no one had been knocked out at all, and I
had demolished my fingernails for nothing. Still, said Chris, at
least the standard would be higher in the second round, as all

the duff teams would be knocking each other out in the plate competition. Terence said he felt particularly hopeful about the second round. Really, I said, on what grounds? No, not confident we would win, said Terence, just confident he would be able to turn up. Oh, well, thank you, I said. We waited eagerly to hear who our opponents would be. With luck we would be playing a side nearer to home. Or we could be travelling even further afield, maybe to the wilds of Bounds Green.

On Monday the phone call came. Away to a pub in Muswell Hill. 'Hmm,' said Chris. 'Rough pub.' Immediately I imagined bodies flying through the air, chairs being smashed over heads, and Chris, George, Terence and me sitting quietly in the corner trying to remember which was the only Sweet single to reach number one.[1] George told me later that Chris has a tendency to say 'Hmm, rough pub' about any pub he hasn't ever been into. That way no one is disappointed. After Finsbury Park, though, we were feeling reasonably confident. Even flying chairs would be no threat if we moved quickly enough.

On Wednesday afternoon, as I was psyching myself up for the forthcoming contest by watching *Ready Steady Cook*, the phone rang. It was Tanja from the Prince of Wales. The competition's organisers had just rung her. There was a change of plan. We would not be playing the Muswell Hill pub this evening; instead we would be going somewhere in Crouch End. 'Hmm, rough pub,' said Chris when I phoned to tell him. In truth, none of us were too concerned. Muswell Hill, Crouch End: what did it matter? Our preparations continued. I considered meditation, massage and yoga before plumping for a medium deep pan Hawaiian with extra cheese.

---

[1] Blockbuster.

At 6:30 the phone rang again. It was Tanja again. There was another change of plan. We were playing the Muswell Hill pub after all. I rang my team-mates' answering machines. All three were still on their way home from work. It would be a miracle if they all managed to pick up their messages and went to the right place in time for the first question at 8:30. Assuming, that is, that the venue hadn't been changed again between now and then.

Half an hour later, Tanja rang a third time. We would not be playing the Muswell Hill pub, nor would we be playing the Crouch End pub, or any pub anywhere tonight, as the fixture had been cancelled. We had a bye through to the next round. We had won by default.

Muswell Hill and Crouch End, we learned later, had played each other the previous week. There had been a disagreement over the scores. Muswell Hill thought they had won. Crouch End considered victory to be theirs. Whether chairs had been thrown we never found out, but we agreed that it was far more fun to speculate that they might have been than confirm that they hadn't been. With barely an hour and a half to go, and no sign of the dispute being settled, the organisers had taken the difficult decision to defer their decision indefinitely. Muswell Hill and Crouch End would be packed off to arbitration, possibly at the UN, and we would move on to round three. Well, said Chris, at least we can say we got there first.

I'd like to say that we were delighted by this, and we were, to some small extent. But the two missing Wednesdays were oddly dispiriting. No one pretends any more, even in the Olympics, that winning matters less than taking part. But winning without taking part really is a waste of time. Sometimes a contestant on *Fifteen-To-One* reaches the last three without answering a single question in round two. Everyone else is so intent on knocking each other out that they forget the Dull Bloke At No. 7, who at first probably can't believe his luck.

But I bet he would have preferred to take part properly, and if possible to have reached the final on his merits, if he had any. That first Wednesday the four of us sat in the pub feeling victorious but a little deflated.

Still, we were through to the last 64, a phrase we now realised was only half as magical and wondrous as 'the last 32'. In round three we were drawn away to the Cricklewood Hotel, a huge rambling pub on the perilous borders of Kilburn. 'Go west, young man!' said John L B Soule, editor of the *Terre Haute Express* (Indiana), in 1851, although it's just possible he may have been talking about something else. So we piled into a mini-cab and rattled around the North Circular, playfully cracking our knuckles and trying to put all thoughts of rogue anagrams out of our minds. After our fortnight off we feared we might be ring rusty. Since the first round none of us had been attending the Tuesday night quiz as regularly, either because we feared that too much quizzing would dull our competitive edge, or because we couldn't be bothered. There were other things to do of an evening. Too much quizzing can make Jack a dull boy, often with an unconvincing ponytail. So we were a little more anxious than we probably needed to be, which is to say that Chris wasn't anxious at all, while I busily consumed what was left of my fingernails in lieu of dinner.

The pub, vast, labyrinthine and dominated at all angles by overhead football, was almost deserted, so we found a table and sat with our drinks, waiting to be spotted by our hosts. Terence, an avid trencherman in normal circumstances, studied the menu, which was full of life-shortening fried things with extra chips. Fortunately he was too nervous to eat (he claimed to be too full from lunch). A few minutes after eight, a nearby table was occupied by four likely-looking characters, three male and one female, all in their early forties. They had an Indefinable Air of Quiz about them. I wondered whether we should go over and say hello. George said we should wait for them to come and say hello to us. It was their pub, after all. We remained in our seats, and drank slightly more quickly.

At about 8:20, just after Newcastle United had conceded a goal, I could bear it no longer. I stood up and ambled over.

'Hello,' I said breezily, 'are you our opponents tonight?'

'We certainly are,' said the woman with some relief.

'Nice place, this,' I ventured politely. 'Very comfortable.'

'Yes, isn't it?' said the woman.

'So what's the form? Usual sort of thing?' I asked.

'Well, you should know,' said the woman, with a grimace.

Before I could reply, a man with an Indefinable Air of Landlord wandered up.

'You must be here for the quiz,' he said to me, for perhaps I had an Indefinable Air of Quiz about me too. I signalled to my team-mates, who swung into action, picking up their coats, drinks and general detritus with palpable enthusiasm. Rarely had I seen them so animated. They had been discussing the menu, and had reasoned, in the event correctly, that the half-time snacks would be something special.

We followed the landlord through another cavernous bar area where you could have staged a perfectly reasonable game of five-a-side football, to a small secluded platform at the front of the pub. Here sat four people who were not the four people I had just met. A huge, ursine character in his mid-forties stood up and proffered a paw.

'You must be the Prince of Wales,' he said.

'We certainly are.'

'Er, excuse me,' said the woman who had been sitting on the other side of the bar, and had followed us through. 'We're the Prince of Wales.'

'What?' said I.

'No. Surely not,' said George.

'Looks very much like it,' said Chris.

'We're from the Prince of Wales,' said the woman, again. 'In Enfield.[2] We are supposed to be playing here tonight. Look.' She thrust into my hand the list of third-round matches that had been sent to all surviving entrants. Three of the entrants were called 'The Prince of Wales'. Only one was supposed to be playing the Cricklewood Hotel tonight. George laughed. If you can call it a laugh. The home team sat stock still.

'Aren't there any addresses on the list?' asked Terence, reasonably enough. 'Is there any way of distinguishing between all these Princes of Wales?'

But there were no addresses, just seven-digit entrant numbers listed beside the pub names. Which could so easily be misread, or misinterpreted.

'We'll just have to ring Burns & Porter,' said Chris. 'They should be able to sort it out. There's a number on the sheet to ring in case of emergencies.'

I found 20p. This whole magnificent fiasco should indeed be easy to resolve, once we knew whose entrant number was whose. Either we or the other Prince of Wales had made a dreadful mistake. The woman from the other Prince of Wales, whose mouth had now tightened as though pulled by drawstrings, was sure that it wasn't them. I wasn't so sure that it wasn't us. Tanja had told us we were going to the Cricklewood Hotel, and we had taken her word for it. Fortunately no one tried to accompany me to the pub's payphone, which was on the other side of one of the more distant bars, comfortably out of earshot of this awkward scene.

There is a sensation that passes through your stomach at

---

[2] Names have been changed to protect innocent boroughs.

such moments, pitched somewhere between pins and needles
and the after-effects of swallowing bleach. It's much the same
feeling I have frequently enjoyed when being fired from jobs
or dumped by girlfriends: an overpowering sense of impending
doom followed, with brutal speed, by the doom itself. The
young woman on the end of the line at Burns & Porter obviously felt the same way. 'Oh my God,' she said when I told
her what had happened. 'Er, hold the line a minute.'

It was now 8:28. If we had cocked it up, and we were supposed to be in Tufnell Park or Kensal Rise tonight, there
wouldn't be time to phone the right pub, let alone drive there.
Reading the fixture list again, I noticed that two of the similarly named pubs were down as 'Prince of Wales', while the
one supposed to be playing the Cricklewood Hotel was 'The
Prince of Wales'. Had we awarded ourselves a definite article
we did not deserve?

'Okay, right, I have it on the screen here,' said the young
woman on the end of the line. 'The Cricklewood Hotel . . .
tappity-tap against . . . *tappity-tap* The Prince of Wales . . . *tap*
Highgate High Street, London N6.' This was us. I breathed for
the first time in what felt like several minutes. 'Thanks very
much,' I said. 'Could you hold the line for a moment?'

I raced back, trying not to grin. The other team were
explaining themselves. They had seen the name 'The Prince of
Wales' opposite the Cricklewood Hotel on the fixtures list and
assumed it was them because the last three digits of the entrant
number were also the street number of their pub. Well, why
not? But it was mere coincidence: the entrant number was ours
and street numbers had nothing to do with it. They had read
significance into coincidence, and so driven miles out of their
way to the wrong pub, when they should now be in Kensal
Rise or Tufnell Park or somewhere else. I gave them the
good news. They were not pleased.

'So what are we supposed to do now?' asked the youngest of

the three men. This was a hard question to answer. 'Sod off' came immediately to mind, but etiquette demanded a gentler response. The woman, drawstring mouth pulled even tighter, went off to confirm my news with Burns & Porter on the payphone. She came back and nodded sadly. They left in silent fury. They obviously felt they had been tricked in some way. Whether they reached the correct destination, or just went home, we never found out.

After all this the quiz was almost an anticlimax. If anything, our overwhelming sense of relief at being at the right place playing the right team worked to our advantage, and we finished the first leg with a nine point lead. One pair of questions on motoring, though, did illustrate the importance of blind good fortune when taking part in a Burns & Porter quiz.

Question A (to them): Which country has the international car registration letters SF?

Answer: Finland. (The S is for Suomi, the Finnish name for Finland.) This is quite an easy one, which comes up more often than frequently in pub quizzes.

Question B (to us): Before which year must a car have been made to be classified as vintage?

Answer: 1930. This is not an easy one, and unlike the other question, totally unguessable if you don't know it. Which of course we didn't. Bitter, over two points lost in an otherwise comfortable victory, nearly a year ago? Me?

We won the second leg no less comfortably. All the bad luck went the Cricklewood's way, including a particularly wriggly individual round question (on the Joker) about Sir Alec Douglas-Home. The poor bloke who was supposed to be answering it came from New Zealand, where Sir Alec had obviously made a less than lasting impression. So we moved into the last 32, and a home tie against the Prince George of

Cumberland, NW1. Even the name sounded fearsome. 'Hmm, obscure pub,' said Chris, who had never heard of it.[3]

This lot, though, looked like quizzers. Unequivocally short-sighted, and wearing sweaters simultaneously drab and over-patterned, the Prince George of Cumberland team had clearly done this sort of thing before. One of their four wore a knitted tie and looked like A J P Taylor. Another scraped perhaps seven hairs across a broad cranium, even though he was only about thirty-five. None of them looked you in the eye. They were terrifying.

And we didn't even have the comforting presence of Chris to console us. Some months ago he had picked this week to go on holiday; now we were cursing his name. Michael couldn't make it either – his father-in-law was in hospital, his pregnant wife was moving office and the two of them had to move house at the weekend (not very impressive excuses, if you ask me) – so George suggested his girlfriend Lesley, who, despite only occasional appearances on the quiz circuit, tends towards omniscience. He assured me that she wouldn't let us down, but I was still as jumpy as a jackrabbit. This round would be a real test of our temperament. Vast quizzing minds were ranged against us. Would we have the intellectual resources and poor dress sense to compete?

Fortunately Terence was sporting one of the nastier woollen items he picked up for a song at Wembley Market several decades ago. We could fight dirty too. But our star was Lesley. She played a blinder, supplying several inspired

---

[3] He was Queen Anne's husband, and served as her Lord High Admiral (or 'love slave') until he died in 1708. Just to show that breweries never get it right, he should correctly be referred to as either 'Prince George of Denmark' or 'the Duke of Cumberland', but not 'Prince George of Cumberland'. A pint of lager top and a packet of Mini-Cheddars, please.

answers to questions that were appreciably harder than those in previous rounds. Which 1974 disco favourite features the line, 'Anybody could be that guy, the night is young and the music's high'?[4] Nails have, in a broad sense, a similar composition to hair. From what fibrous structural protein are both made?[5] In the Middle Ages the practice of 'simony' was widespread, involving the buying and selling of what?[6]

We still needed the Prince George team to make mistakes, and amazingly they did. Popular culture was their weakness. They failed to identify the names of two (then) new albums by the Lighthouse Family and Ocean Colour Scene;[7] and they faltered on the title of a particularly rank comedy film that had just come out. George knows everything there is to be known about pop music, and I remembered the name of the film, which meant lots of lovely bonus points for us.

They made one particularly grave cock-up. It was the individual round of the bloke looking like A J P Taylor, and the subject was Games. AJP looked confident, even smug. He knew that there are seven possible opening moves in draughts, and that Alfred M Butts invented Scrabble. Tanja read out his question. How many male characters are featured in the original version of the board game Cluedo? This was cleverly phrased: the words 'original version' implied that the game had been drastically altered at some stage since. It hasn't, of

---

[4] 'Dancing Queen' by Abba.
[5] Keratin.
[6] Church pardons and offices. The name derives from Simon Magus, who did a lot of it in the reign of Nero. According to Hippolytus, he offered to be buried alive, and promised to reappear on the third day. He was buried in a deep trench, 'but to this day,' says Hippolytus, 'his disciples have failed to witness his resurrection.'
[7] *Postcards From Heaven*; *Marchin' Already*. I wouldn't have got them either.

course, but during an individual round you are apt to forget your own name if not frequently reminded of it. Poor AJP panicked. He knew there were four if you counted Dr Black, the murder victim. Everybody else in the pub knew there were four. Everybody else in the pub knew he was going to say three. And he did. Four points lost; two extra points gained by us.

It shows just how tight these contests can be. They were a highly impressive bunch, with a broad sweep of knowledge stored in huge skulls. We were on top form, dredging up the more difficult answers and not making a single mistake on the more straightforward questions. They knew nothing about current pop music or films released the previous Friday. And yet, after eight rounds, we were still only nine points ahead. It sounds comfortable enough, but we knew at heart that they were at least as good as us, and potentially rather better. The last 32: still only half as magical as the last 16.

The second leg, Wednesday 19 November 1997, in the Prince George of Cumberland, Albany Street, NW1. It's a quiet, almost incongruous pub, positioned apparently randomly on a charmless through-route tucked behind the whitewashed splendour of Regent's Park. Some boozers thrive in the most unlikely circumstances, and this one seems to despite the absence of any obvious clientele. When we arrive a handful of elderly and suspicious Irishmen are scattered around the bar, and satellite basketball booms from an overhead TV. But the joint is hardly a-jumpin'. Over the road lies the Regent's Park Barracks, which may or may not be on full-time alert in case the Russians change their minds and decide to invade after all. You would never know it in any case: the building is shrouded in institutional darkness and scrupulously guarded by soldiers who regard all pedestrians as a grave threat to national security. As a result virtually no one walks the street, and yet this

400-yard-long thoroughfare somehow supports five pubs. The economics of drink remain a mystery to us all.

We are, at least, back at full strength, although after Lesley's performance last week we aren't sure what that means any more. We order our drinks and drift towards the largest table, staking out our territory while pretending that we are not doing anything of the sort. There are newspapers here to leaf through: these provide excellent cover. Our opponents arrive. They look more confident on home turf, as you might expect. They are also not quite the same team. Two of last week's players have been dropped, or perhaps they couldn't make it, or perhaps they were only substitutes for the two who have replaced them this week. There is no way of knowing, so the mind fills the gaps with anxiety and paranoia. Their obvious shyness makes them even more formidable. They are still not looking us in the eye, while we are straining to be friendly and matter-of-fact. You would never guess that it was us who won 57–48 only a week ago. We settle into the designated quizzing tables, while the quizmaster squeezes a little too cosily between us. A J P Taylor tucks a tattered Piers Anthony paperback into his jacket pocket. George grimaces. Terence roots around for a spare biro. The quizmaster rips open the plastic covering which contains this week's questions, and prepares to read.

It is instantly clear that this will be a more even contest. The scores are 7-all after round one, 14-all after round two, 23-all after round three, the first individual round. Again and again the Prince George threatens to build a lead; each time we somehow claw our way back. After round four it's half-time. The Prince George lead 28 to 27.

The landlord brings out the food, which mainly consists of large chunks of roast pork and sliced white Mother's Pride. (A single lettuce leaf decorates the main platter, representing nutrition.) We are still eight points ahead, and we are holding

our own. So why are we the nervous ones? Because already we
have made one or two foolish errors, and we constantly
threaten to make more. We are desperate to reach the last 16 –
and, if anything, more so after AJP tells me that this may be
the last qualifying round. If previous years are anything to go
by, the last 16 from the main cup competition and the last four
from the sad 'plate' competition will move straight on to the
Grand Final. (I can hear those initial capital letters in his
voice as he describes it.) The Prince George reached the
Grand Final last year, he adds with a smile. How did you do?
I ask. Not bad, he says, waiting for me to ask him more. I say
nothing.

The last four rounds, the last 16 questions. At this stage,
defending a narrow lead, a football manager would take off his
attacking midfield player and his goal-hungry star striker and
put on a couple of burly defenders with broken noses and bad
tempers to make sure the other team didn't get any big ideas.
I look round at Terence, who is absently munching crisps.
Suddenly our resources seem frighteningly meagre.

But let's not blame Terence, for it is I who starts getting
answers wrong. In my individual round – Science – I am
given a long, technical and intentionally confusing definition
of what sounds like a sonic boom. What is it? Like AJP a
week before, I panic. I think the answer might be sonic boom,
but I am suddenly paralysed by the thought that if it's not, I
am going to look a fool. This is the brilliance of the individual round, which turns us all into inmates of Dotheboys
Hall, forever in fear of humiliation and punishment. If I get
this wrong, (a) I will not look a fool; (b) even if I do, no one
will remember in five minutes; and (c) there are only eight
other people here, five of whom I will probably never see
again. None of this matters. So instead of saying 'sonic boom'
(which is the right answer) I say nothing, and throw away
more points.

Somehow we hang on. After round seven the Prince George lead 50 to 47. We have a 6-point cushion. Surely we are safe now. I begin to smile, and even breathe from time to time as well. Round eight, question 1. Motor racing: Formula One, 1997. What is the name of the bend on the Grand Prix circuit at Jerez where, a week or two ago, Michael Schumacher so elegantly attempted to run Jacques Villeneuve out of the race? 'Bend?' I think. 'Bend? He wants us to name a bend? Why not just ask us the name of Villeneuve's favourite football team, or Schumacher's accountant?' Needless to say we don't know the answer,[8] but the Prince George do, and they also know the answer to their own, much easier question (Who won that Grand Prix at Jerez?[9]). We are now only three points ahead, with three pairs of questions left.

The next pair of questions are on poetry. 'Which poem begins "The curfew tolls the knell of parting day"?' 'Gray's "Elegy in a Country Churchyard",' says Chris. Two points. 'Which poem begins "Quinquireme of Nineveh from distant Ophir"?' '"Cargoes",' say the Prince George. Two points. We're still 3 ahead, with two pairs of questions to go. It only needs one mistake. Next up, Firsts in Aviation History. This could be our downfall. 'Which "air first" was achieved by Jean Pierre Blanchard and Dr John J Jeffries in 1785?' Our minds empty. We cannot think, or even begin to think. The Prince George think they know. Were they the first to cross the English Channel in the balloon? They were. Bonus point.

The Prince George's turn. 'Which "air first" was achieved by Captain Ross Smith in 1919?' Chris is trying to pretend he knows the answer to this, when it's obvious he doesn't. Lose the initiative, and we'll lose the game. The Prince George rack

---

[8] The Dry Sack Curve.
[9] Mika Hakkinen.

their gigantic brains. Terence thinks he can see the individual veins throbbing. For the first time in this long and agonising match they have a chance to win, and you can see their confidence slipping away as though it had a prior engagement. They don't know the answer, and neither do we.[10] We are 2 points ahead overall. Each team has one question left.

Dead, heavy silence, finally interrupted by the quizmaster clearing his throat. If you were setting this quiz, would you end with an easy one, or a very difficult one, or one that requires specialist knowledge, or a tricksy, stupid one? Please, God, just let it be something we know. The quizmaster reads our question.

'In which successful TV comedy sequel did Bob marry Thelma?'

Thank you, God, for popular culture. '*Whatever Happened to the Likely Lads*,' we chorus, and we are through to the Grand Final. If A J P Taylor had got his Cluedo question right, we would have lost. Fortunately it's some days before this thought occurs to me. We shake hands, say our farewells, grab a cab to the Prince of Wales, tell Tanja the good news and get fantastically pissed.

Answers to Quiz 8

The item that was discovered yards away from the bridge of the *Titanic*, which might have saved 1,523 lives had it been used, was a pair of binoculars. Leofric, Earl of Mercia, who

---

[10] Captain Smith was the first pilot to fly from England to Australia. It took him (and his brother, who navigated) 28 days to make the trip, and when they landed in Darwin they were both knighted for their trouble. Presumably they had sent Lloyd George the cheque in advance.

died in 1057, was also Lord of Coventry, and his wife was better known as Lady Godiva. The song 'Gwendolyne' came fourth in the Eurovision Song Contest of 1970; the singer, representing Spain, was Julio Iglesias. The longest river wholly in England is the Thames. Paul Gascoigne, when asked on live Norwegian TV before a Norway-England World Cup qualifier if he had a message for the Norwegian people, said 'Fuck off Norway'.

Quiz 9

• What was introduced to the FA Cup Final in 1927 at the bidding of Queen Mary?
• An American state, an American city, a precious metal, a Roman goddess and a weapon. What's the connection?
• In which village does Rupert Bear live?
• In English law, what is the smallest number of people that can constitute a riot?
• What is the hierarchical system in domestic chickens called?

15
In With the Big Boys

'The horror! The horror!'

(Kurtz in Joseph Conrad's *Heart of Darkness*)

The Grand Final of the *Evening Standard* Pub Quiz Challenge was held on 4 March 1998, at the Old Town Hall, Kings Road in Chelsea. It's a distinctive part of town, traditionally populated by the rich, the fashionable, the young and the thin – which made it pretty easy to spot most of the contestants, as they shambled up from Sloane Square Tube in their Competition Knitwear. Quizzers are more likely to be unnecessarily early for an appointment than any other sector of the population, so at 6:45, a full fifteen minutes before we were even allowed to enter the building, a few sorry men were already loitering on the pavement outside, wondering what to do. Among them, rather sheepishly, were George and I, who had already had a drink at a pub down the road. The only sensible solution was to go for another drink at another pub down another road. On the way we bumped into our supersub Michael, who with Tanja would constitute our support for the evening. In a second-hand bookshop Michael had just bought *Intimate Sex Lives of Famous People*, which impressed George no end. This slightly stained volume was just what we needed to take our minds off the forthcoming contest. By the time we eventually rolled into the Old Town Hall, we were pleasantly relaxed.

In this, it seemed, we were alone. Teams had begun to congregate in a makeshift bar in a back room of the Hall, and were already eyeing each other suspiciously. In the middle stood Chris, Terence and Tanja, cradling glasses of cheap red wine and looking as out of place as undertakers at a wedding. Three months had passed since the last qualifying round – more than long enough for our elation to wither and be displaced by a sense of serious foreboding. Our win at the Prince George of Cumberland had been glorious but fortunate. Those had been no mere amateurs we had beaten. Those had been hardened quizzing professionals. And here, standing around us, were nineteen more teams of hardened professionals, several of whom had science fiction novels crammed into their jacket pockets. Here were the quizzing aristocracy, decked out in their ceremonial plumage and regalia. 'Good evening,' said George to our team-mates. 'Is it?' said Chris.

Fortunately one man looked even more nervous and uncomfortable than we did. Henry Kelly, our questionmaster for the evening, stood in the least populated area of the room, clearly hoping that no one would pluck up the courage to go and talk to him. To this end the former host of *Going For Gold* gallantly concentrated his attentions on an attractive young woman, who, being attractive, young and a woman, rather stood out from the quizzing crowd.

The drinks, it turned out, were free. This was no small consolation. 'Just as long as we don't come last,' said George for the third time. 'I figure eleventh is as much as we can hope for,' said Chris. 'Just below halfway. Never in with a shout, but avoiding complete humiliation.'

'Is that Danny Baker over there?' said George. No, but whoever it was could have made a useful living as a lookalike. 'Does the world need a Danny Baker lookalike?' said Michael.

Kelly had replaced the original host, Robert Powell. We had all been intrigued by the prospect of a pub quiz hosted by Jesus Christ. 'Never mind,' said George, 'at least Donald Yule is here.'

'Who?' said Terence.

'Where? Where?' said I.

'Donald Yule. Frequent *Fifteen-To-One* grand finalist. Over there by the window. I knew you'd be interested,' said George, cruelly.

'Well, it's a different sort of celebrity, isn't it, *Fifteen-To-One* celebrity,' said I. Terence's eyes glazed over.

'I tell you, there's at least one beard a team here,' said Michael. 'I saw that bloke on *Mastermind*,' said George. 'Or perhaps it was *Crimewatch*.'

Michael said his wife had recently spotted an old teacher on a TV quiz show. Several years ago this teacher had been accused of interfering with pupils, although obviously he had neglected to mention this to the programme's researchers. 'Pity it wasn't on *Countdown*,' I said. ' "Paedophile" would make a terrific *Countdown* conundrum.'

'Except that it's got ten letters,' said George.

' "Pederasts" would do,' said Chris.

Tanja, landlady to the last, pointed out that a majority of contestants were drinking bitter. 'Except all the men in suits,' said Terence. 'They're on red wine.' Thus were class differentials established and confirmed. 'I tell you, that's Danny Baker,' said George.

'Catamites,' said Chris. 'That's got nine letters too.'

A man with a reedy voice asked us all to move into the main hall. The quiz, he said, would commence in fifteen min-

utes. (Most quizzes just begin or start. We felt honoured to be
at one that was about to commence.) Most teams rushed
straight through, programmed by years of pub quizzes to try to
secure the best table. We were more reluctant to move. We
knew we had a table reserved for us. We suspected that drinks
would continue to be free, although Terence kept glancing
around in case someone leapt out of the shadows and presented him with a bill. We felt in no great hurry. We liked
winning too much to come 17th, which we all silently believed
to be our fate.

Eventually we trudged into the main hall. Subdued and
fatalistic we might have been, but even we had to marvel at
its impressive dimensions. Chelsea Old Town Hall was built
in 1886 and is of the municipal triumphalism school of architecture. Its main hall, into which you could fit at least one
run-down housing estate, is decorated by murals portraying
Chelsea's association with the arts, literature and science.
These were painted by artists chosen in open competition in
1912. Two years later, after much discussion, the Borough
Council voted to take down the mural depicting literature
because it contained a portrait of Oscar Wilde. Shortly afterwards war broke out, and the resolution was forgotten. Oscar
has stayed there ever since, staring down lasciviously at generations of young Chelsea manhood. We can only guess what
he might have made of the teams taking part that evening in
the Grand Final of the *Evening Standard* Pub Quiz Challenge.

The event's organisers had tried hard to live up to the
grandeur of the surroundings. Twenty small tables, numbered
and diplomatically well spaced, were arranged in front of a
wide, raised platform of a type you might expect to see at a
minor awards dinner, or possibly the annual conference of an
unsuccessful political party. Two young women in identical
suits sat behind a console, clutching biros. Huge logos adorned
an extravagant central backdrop. On either side, two even

broader white boards displayed the names of the twenty competing pubs, all printed in a suitably authoritative typeface. One unmarked area looked as though it might have doubled as a video screen. I caught Chris's eye. It had a tear in it. Here it was at last: the questionmaster's table of our dreams. For years we had made do with an old microphone with a loose connection, and a table with one leg marginally shorter than the others, so that drinks always slopped over the answer sheets. This was the same sort of thing, only designed by NASA. It was extraordinary to think that it had been built for one night only, at a fair cost, for this event, for us. The contrast with the mean little tables we were all perched at was striking. Everyone sat in awed silence, shuffling piles of rough paper and feeling a little silly.

Waitresses came round with beautifully arranged and expertly cooked sausages and mash. It must have cost the *Evening Standard* a small fortune, and tasted just like sausages and mash. Donald Yule walked over and gave us a flyer for a competition organised by the South London Quiz League. 'Lots of weird people here tonight,' he said, and wandered off. 'Did he mean us?' said George.

A man stood up to introduce us to ourselves. We had all seen the lists of competitors, and sneered at each other in the bar. Nonetheless he announced each team in turn, to muted cheers from each team's two supporters, who had all been herded to larger tables at the back of the hall. 'This is embarrassing,' said George. Each team was reduced to cheering itself. One or two cheered with rather too much gusto. 'They're pissed,' said Chris. Obviously we hadn't been the only team to guzzle down the beer in case it ran out. Even when there's a trophy to play for, and the chance to shake hands with a famous newspaper editor, an Englishman's eyes light up at the prospect of free drink.

A man from the Lord's Taverners stood up to speak. The venerable cricket charity was this evening's main beneficiary.

'Very very briefly,' he began, 'this is what we are all about.' It
wasn't brief enough. Attentions were wandering. Finally he
mentioned Henry Kelly. 'A man who needs no introduction,' he
said, before giving him one anyway. Our host trotted up to the
stage and, inspired by the previous speaker, rambled on for ages.
On Classic FM that morning he had been fast and fluent, but
now, after a long and exhausting day, he was slow and deliberate, taking care to pronounce every consonant, some of them
more than once.

'This should be fun,' said George.

There were eight rounds, each of seven questions, with one
point per question, and the occasional bonus to be had if you
were on the ball. 'Round one is General Knowledge,' said
Henry. Rounds two to eight would turn out to be as well.

1 What will a team of Russian divers be looking for over
   the coast of Cornwall in June 1998?
2 What is the strongest known natural fibre?
3 How old will Lenny Henry and Michael Jackson be on
   their birthdays on 29 August 1998?
4 The Daimler Conquest saloon of 1953–8 was so-called
   because its price before British Purchase Tax was
   originally how much?
5 The Rubik's cube consists of how many smaller coloured
   cubes that rotate on a central axis?
6 Theresa, who appeared in *Coronation Street* at the end of
   1997 before her character was killed off, recently went
   missing. Who or what was Theresa?
7 What is remarkable about the spelling of the place name
   Llareggub, the fictional Welsh town in which *Under Milk
   Wood* is set?

Don't worry, I won't print them all, but I thought you might
like a flavour of the questions we had to answer. What struck us

immediately was that these were all very gettable. Question 1 had to be Atlantis: what else could it be? Question 2, Terence thought, was a spider's web. Question 3 had to be forty: again, if it were not a nice round answer, why ask the question? Question 4, for exactly the same reason, was presumably £1,066. Question 5 was the number of smaller cubes in a 3×3×3 cube, minus one for the central axis: that is, 26. Now to question 6. 'A dog?' said Terence. 'A turkey,' said Chris. 'Trust me.' We trusted him. And question 7, we knew, spelt 'Bugger All' backwards.

We had not wanted to be there. We had been moaning and drinking and moping and absolutely certain that we were going to make fools of ourselves. Yet as soon as the first question was asked our competitive spirit kicked in and all doubts were vanquished. We were fairly certain of 5 of these 7. Terence had good feelings about spider's web, and Chris had the Gleam of Certainty on turkey. Suddenly the horror did not seem quite so acute. Meanwhile, Henry Kelly was moving straight on to round two. Answers would be read out and scores updated after every second round.

Round two was called Name the Year. Questions 1 to 6 were about events from a particular year. Question 7, for three points, asked you to name the year. The first 6 were, again, highly gettable. Who fed his four-year-old daughter a beefburger in front of journalists, to show beef was safe to eat?[1] Which tiny footballing nation beat Austria 1–0 in their first international match?[2] The year was more of a problem. This was the year in which *Dances With Wolves* had been released, in which Helen Sharman had become Britain's first astronaut. We plumped for 1991.

---

[1] John Selwyn Gummer, then Minister of Agriculture.
[2] Faroe Islands.

We were wrong. It was 1990. Amazingly, though, we had
got every other question in the first two rounds right. We were
slightly overwhelmed. With 13 out of 16 points, we were also
first equal.

Round three was Sport. Which is the only football club to
win an FA Cup Final without an Englishman in their team?[3]
Which is the fastest of all court games?[4] Incredibly, George
knew both of these. (Terence and I, who had contributed little
so far, just bowed down and chanted 'We are not worthy'.)
Round four was the Audio round: 7 questions about music or
the spoken word that could show off Chelsea Old Town Hall's
sound system. Most satisfying of these was a clip from *Porridge*,
with David Jason playing Blanco. It wasn't immediately obvious, but we recognised it. At the halfway mark, with full marks
in each of these rounds (full marks! us!), we were on 27 points
out of a possible 30. Four teams were second equal on 23. This
was not what we had expected.

Different pressures were now coming into play. We had
never contemplated victory. We had only ever wanted to
avoid making total tits of ourselves. Now, after a stream of
questions that appeared to have been geared to the precise
limits of our knowledge, we had a chance to win: indeed,
probably the best chance to win. From no-hopers to ante-post
favourites in just over an hour . . . if this had been professional sport, the Drug Squad would have been called in.
Some observers might have regarded my frequent visits to
the lavatory with suspicion, had they not clocked my unnerv-
ing lager consumption. My bladder was less impressed than
anyone.

On to round five, the Anagram round. The first letters of

---

[3] Liverpool, when they beat Everton 3–1 in 1986.
[4] Pelota.

the answers to questions 1 to 6 formed an anagram of the answer to question 7. One point for questions 1 to 6, three for question 7. The clue to question 7 was as follows: Britain's one was once in the pink, but not any more. 'Empire,' said Chris. Yes, of course; so now we could go back and work out the others we hadn't known. Even then we made a couple of mistakes. Which is the world's most isolated city? We just couldn't think, although we thought it started with the letter M. We wasted ages trying to think of cities beginning with M – whereas if we had been thinking of cities beginning with P, we might have been in with a chance.[5]

Round six was the *Evening Standard* round, a sop to placate the sponsors and annoy all those participants who read the paper as infrequently as possible. In 1998 the *Evening Standard* was advertising Barry Manilow concerts with the line 'Ever wondered why your parents called you . . .' what?[6] What activity was the Duchess of York doing one-handed on the front page of a recent (March 1998) edition of the *Evening Standard*? George's response was unrepeatable; fortunately Terence knew the real answer.[7]

Three quarters of the way through, we had 41 out of a possible 46. Three teams had 38, three more 37. We couldn't afford to slip up. So far we had been lucky. Wild guesses had come off, some questions we had correctly worked out, and many we had simply known. There's no great mystery to it.

---

[5] Perth in Australia. It's so far from anywhere that the nearest city is in South Africa.

[6] Mandy. Looking around at the other teams, we couldn't imagine that any of their parents had christened them Mandy. (Although it's possible that one or two may have called themselves that in their spare time.)

[7] Ski-ing.

We were in the lead because we had not made a single stupid mistake. There were only two rounds to go. We had to keep concentrating.

Round seven was called Links. The answers to questions 1 to 6 were all linked in some way; question 7 asked you to guess the connection. This, we agreed, was the most ingenious round in the competition, so I shall renege on my previous promise, and reproduce it here in full.

1 Who or what was 'On the Moon' for REM in the 1992 pop charts?
2 Which word is most frequently used in English conversation?
3 Which property of a body is measured in Newtons?
4 At the end of which 1997 thriller did Brad Pitt receive his wife's head in a box?
5 In *Star Trek: The Next Generation*, what is the name of Lt. Commander Data's cat?
6 What name is given to a store of potatoes buried under straw or earth in an open field or garden?
7 What connects the answers to the last six questions?

From the beginning: question 1 George and I both knew was 'Man'. Question 2: was it 'the'? Leave this one for the time being. Question 3 we knew was 'force'. Question 4 Chris and Terence both recognised as *Seven*. (Any closer to the link yet?) Question 5 I knew I knew, but the drink was beginning to affect me now, and I couldn't remember it. Question 6 we didn't know at all.

Hmm. Question 2: could it be 'I'? George was sure that either 'the' or 'and' was the most frequently used word in the written language, but how could they be connected with the others? 'Man', 'force', 'seven', 'the' or 'and' or 'I'. Hmm.

Serious panic now. Seconds ticking away. What was the

name of Data's fucking cat? I know it's ginger, for Christ's sake. Oh shitfuckbollockswank. Have watched far too many episodes of *Star Trek* for my own good. Must be able to remember this.

No progress on other questions, or on the link. Opinions hardening on 'I' for question 2. Inspiration urgently required. Spot. Data's cat is called Spot. Where does such information come from? Where has it been hiding? But I know it's right.

And George instantly works out the link: the letter G. G-man, G.I., G-force, G-7 and, of course, G-spot. And one other we didn't know. Which turned out to be G-clamp, which I'm sure you got paragraphs ago. Only one point dropped.

The final round was a picture round, to justify the expense of that back projection screen. (No videos, sadly, or close-ups of Henry Kelly.) Here, inevitably, we fell to earth. A photograph of a cathedral. No, don't recognise it. A photograph of a sportsman with a moustache. Sorry, try another one. We knew three or four of the seven, but the teams on our tail would have done better than that.

The scores were counted. Teams relaxed, or pretended to. Terence nibbled his pencil. We didn't say much. A pub quiz is such a sociable event. People chat and banter and argue and agree and disagree and take huge offence and forget about it in two minutes. We just sat and drank. Finally Henry Kelly was reactivated and the scores were read out in reverse order.

We couldn't have been lower than 4th. Amazing, really: two hours ago, 11th had been our best hope. We would have been delighted with 4th. Not now, though.

In 4th: not us. In 3rd place, with a lower score than we thought we had . . . not us. Unbearable tension. Slurp slurp guzzle slurp.

In second place, with one point less than we thought we had scored, which is to say exactly the number of points we thought we had scored if we had been unlucky about one particular

question . . . The Plough from Worcester Park. All praise ye
Ploughmen you wonderful human beings we may yet snog you
drunkenly a little later although probably not as at least one of
you has a beard . . . for we have won. We have won. Will I trip
on the stairs up to the platform? Will I throw up over the
Editor of the *Evening Standard*?

The next few seconds pass in a deafening blur, as all four
of us find ourselves up on the platform, shaking various hands
and, in my case at least, holding a gaudy trophy aloft as
though it were the FA Cup. We have answered enough
bloody questions about it over the years, so it seems only
appropriate to hold up something vaguely resembling it and
wait for the cheers. Amazingly, people oblige.

Victory: can you beat it? As the reporter for the *Standard*
later wrote:

> *'Marcus Berkmann, a writer and former* Daily Mail
> *television critic, ruefully admitted: "I entered the quiz because
> I'm writing a book about quizzes and I needed a backbone for
> the book. It never occurred to us that we would win." As his
> team-mate George said, helpfully: "It makes it the book of a
> smug bastard."'*

Eventually (i.e. after about five seconds) the applause ceased.
The hall emptied fast. Quizzers don't hang about once they
have lost. No one saw the Editor of the *Evening Standard*
leave: some said it had been faster than the eye could perceive. Soon there were just the four of us left on the stage,
with our cup and our winners' tankards and Henry Kelly, who
was still going strong. The women in identical suits were
bustling around, looking worried. Relax, I thought. It's all
over. We won. What else could possibly matter?

An even more worried-looking man approached us. Could
we join him in the room behind the stage to pose for a few

more photographs? Well, if it's really necessary, of course.
(You want me to pose for more photographs? Show me the
way!)

We filed into the ante-room. The door was closed. The
noise and clamour receded. There was no photographer. All
we could see were the worried-looking women in identical
suits, the worried-looking man and another quiz team (one
beard, grizzled). They looked thoroughly pissed off.

'I'm afraid there's been a terrible mistake,' said the worried-
looking man.

'You bet there's been,' said one of the quizzers.

'I knew we should have stayed in the pub,' said George.

The marking had been cocked up. Apparently the Editor
had been in a hurry to get away and had rushed them along a
bit. (When in doubt blame the boss, especially if he's in a cab
on his way home.) The John Bull in Chiswick had been given
6 for the last round, but had scored 16. Add on the 10 points
they were due, and they were neck-and-neck with us. It was a
tie.

'So we're going to have to have a tie-break,' said Worried-
Looking Man, sweating ferociously.

Silence. I didn't like the idea of this. As Sir Alf Ramsey
once said, 'You've already won it once. Now go out and win
it again.' Easy to say, difficult to achieve. When golfers play
a tie-break at the end of a major championship, it's usually
the one who was chasing the leader who has the advantage.
The poor sod who was leading until the last moment must
call up unfathomable reserves of mental strength to compete
at all. We didn't have unfathomable reserves of mental
strength. We had drunk them hours ago. The John Bull
would be the favourites in such circumstances, inspired as
they would be by the terrible injustice of this one insignifi-
cant arithmetical error. No, a tie-break seemed like a very
bad idea indeed.

'Why don't we just agree to share the prize?' I said.

'Good idea,' said one of the John Bull team, to my amazement. They didn't like the idea either. It was late, we were all exhausted and everybody else had gone home. If they now lost the tie-break, no one would ever know that they had come so close. Earlier they had been denied applause, handshakes and the opportunity to lift the cup in the air. Now they could even be denied second prize, which had already been given to someone else. So it was agreed. The Prince of Wales would keep the trophy for six months, and the John Bull would have it for the other six months. On such capacity for compromise have mighty empires been formed.

'Who gets it first?' said a John Bull man.

'Oh I think we do,' I said. I was holding it at the time, and didn't think I could let go of it.

'And the money for charity? What about that?' said Chris. The winning team also won £2,000 for their favourite charity.

'Well, if you wish you could split that in half, and take £1,000 each,' said Worried-Looking Man. He looked as though someone had pulled his trousers down.

'I have a better idea,' said Chris. 'You can double it. Make it £2,000 for each charity. After all, it's your cock-up.'

'No problem,' said Worried-Looking Man, although his sweat said otherwise. But at least we were all in the clear. New photographs had to be posed, now featuring both winning teams (Prince of Wales muted, John Bull exultant) alongside Henry Kelly, whose stamina was beginning to impress us all. (At least I didn't have my shirt hanging out in these photos. Terence, unfortunately, lifted up his winner's tankard in such a way that his face was completely obscured.) From there it was back to the Prince of Wales for further celebrations. Our long quest for quizzing glory was over. Next year we'll probably be knocked out in the first round.

Answers to Quiz 9

At the bidding of Queen Mary, 'Abide With Me' was first sung at the FA Cup Final of 1927. The American state is Utah, the American city is Omaha, the precious metal is Gold, the Roman goddess is Juno, the weapon is Sword, and together they make up the five D-Day landing beaches in Normandy. Rupert Bear lives in Nutwood. In English law, as few as three people can constitute a riot. And the hierarchical system in domestic chickens is otherwise known as the pecking order.

Quiz 10

- Which is farthest west: Glasgow, Swansea or Plymouth?
- Who was Poet Laureate from 1843 to 1850? (He distinguished himself during his period of office by writing no poetry at all.)
- Which London Underground station has the same name as a station on the Paris Metro?
- What is the Queen's star sign?

And for the last question, a devilish tie-breaker:

- In what year was the first recorded (i.e. written) use of the word 'pig' to describe a policeman?

16
Question or Nominate?

'I've started, so I'll finish.'

(Magnus Magnusson)

Most of *Fifteen-To-One*'s more dedicated viewers will have heard of Trevor Montague. A frequent winner on the show, with the knitwear to match, Trevor qualified for two Grand Finals during 1997 and won one of them. A season or two later, like many high-scorers before him, he grew over-confident and took one too many questions. It's the show's golden rule: concentrate on winning first and think about high scores and Grand Finals later. Over-confidence is regularly punished. To be fair, Trevor, an accountant from Crawley in West Sussex, had never seemed greatly encumbered by modesty. But even he was not immune to the occasional un-answerable question. One such came along, and off he went.

That, we all assumed, was that. A long run on *Fifteen-To-One* is always entertaining to watch, and even more entertaining, I would imagine, to experience yourself. But once you are knocked out, your participation is at an end. The show has a strict rule that no one can enter more than once. You are asked back if you win, or if you are unlucky enough to run into one of the show's very occasional duff questions, when William G Stewart will grant you special dispensation to have another go. Everyone else, though, is barred from re-entering *sine die*, or at least until the show runs out of new contestants and has to allow its veterans back in. When *Mastermind* finally relented and let past contestants re-apply, we knew it was on its last legs. For reasons of credibility if nothing else, *Fifteen-To-One* will resist such a move for as long as possible.

The show has little defence, though, against out-and-out subterfuge. Shortly after Trevor's run, William G and his production company sold several thousand old *Fifteen-To-Ones* to Challenge TV, a cable and satellite channel dedicated to old game and quiz shows. As new channels go it's a remarkable idea, the sort you're glad someone else had. These shows had been mouldering in videotape libraries, or possibly cardboard boxes, for years. Now they are beamed out night and day to audiences that, at their peak, are rumoured to graze double figures.

We know that at least one person was watching on the day Steve Romana took part. Calling himself a 'freelance writer' from Bewbush in West Sussex (a mile or two from Crawley), Steve wore an earring in his right lobe and had slicked back what remained of his hair, as all we freelance writers do. In all other respects, though, he looked exactly like Trevor Montague. Was this an uncanny coincidence? Had identical twins been separated at birth and handed to different adoptive parents? Or had Trevor merely taken off his glasses and entered twice?

What was so curious is that Steve Romana's episode had been recorded in 1992, a full five years before Trevor's Grand Final victory. Why would someone enter under a pseudonym before entering under his own name? Because, as Trevor admitted in court in July 1998, he had already entered as

'Trevor Montague' in 1990, and been knocked out in the first round. Apparently everyone did it in his quiz league. If you don't succeed, try again, as your long-lost identical twin brother from the next road along. Trevor was caught because Challenge TV's viewer contacted Regent Productions and ratted on him. Even then he might have got away with it, had he not contributed to a Channel 4 programme written and hosted by Bob Monkhouse, about the history and practice of TV quiz shows.

Trevor: 'Well, I hope I'm not giving away too many secrets, but on most shows there is a structure to the show. Fifteen-To-One *is one where you have questions that come up again and again and again. Now, when I knew I was going on* Fifteen-To-One, *what I did was tape all the shows . . . I knew what was likely to come up. I knew the areas they may ask me questions on, so I researched them . . . Every question that I'd heard, I'd remembered in my head. I'd watched the tape of the show, I'd made sure they were in my memory. I knew there was a chance that 20 per cent of these questions would be asked me. So it's a big advantage to go in with that edge.'*

Not overtly humble, our Trevor, who told the county court in Wandsworth that to date he had appeared on seventy-three television and radio quiz shows. After the Monkhouse show, William G Stewart and Regent Productions decided to sue him for aggravated damages and the return of his prizes: two goblets, two decanters and a plinth for a vase (which may or may not have been Etruscan). Trevor said he would be counter-suing William G for harassment. 'The memories of winning aren't the same as they were,' he wailed.

Poor Trevor. The words 'hubris' and 'nemesis' immediately come to mind, not least as suitable pseudonyms should he apply again in the future (Dave Hubris, perhaps, and Samantha

Nemesis). Maybe he's right, and thousands of barmy quizzers from West Sussex are appearing on *Fifteen-To-One* over and over again in a series of ever more preposterous wigs. Somehow I doubt it. What I do know is that one person has legitimately appeared twice on *Fifteen-To-One*, without being knocked out in the first round, without winning, without being asked a duff question, and without holding a gun to William G's head in the commercial break. One person, and only one person.

Me.

Let me explain. I had been watching the show for a year or two, idly as you do, then with increasing enthusiasm and finally with that passionate sense of belonging you rarely find outside terrorist organisations. I had to have a go myself. I had to. At the end of his shorter shows, when he has a few minutes spare because the finalists have been crap and answered all the questions wrong, William G Stewart posts up an address to which people like me can send our applications. 'Postcards only, please,' he says sternly, so we send in our postcards of the Algarve or wherever left over from last summer, and are eventually invited to an audition. Mine was in a school hall in Wimbledon in south-west London, and took the form of a game of *Fifteen-To-One*, from which (very kindly) all the more wriggly questions had been excised. The people who knew 0 were weeded out, as was anyone who froze with terror. If you are going to get the screaming heeby-jeebies in a school hall in Wimbledon, then a TV studio in Wandsworth might send you over the edge. I was lucky with my questions, and was one of the last three people left of my fifteen. A week later I received an invitation to a recording of the show. I had passed the audition.

We live in an age in which everyone and his dog has been on television, and the dog has usually been asked back the following week. We all know that (a) it's unbelievably hot in

a TV studio, and you sweat like a pat of butter on a hot
summer's day; (b) everyone looks fat on TV; and (c) people
who work in TV think that what they are doing is the most
important thing in the world, which is the only way they can
stay sane. The *Fifteen-To-One* studio was like any other, which
is to say anonymous and much harder to find than you'd
expect with an up-to-the-minute A-to-Z. Amazingly there
were fifteen of us there, sitting in an ante-room drinking tea
and chomping Lincoln biscuits. William G Stewart
was recording another episode – they do two a day, and
three on Wednesdays – and we watched it on a monitor. Our
previous winner anticipated every answer, in a classic piece of
dressing-room gamesmanship. What was the idea? To
intimidate us, or to provide us with an easy target for our
jealousy and ire?

Nose shine removed, full of biscuits, feeling out of place,
terrified of failure, walking out into the main studio, sense of
impending doom again, why does doom always impend? nothing else does, unbelievably hot, the man in the velvet jacket
may come to regret wearing that, where's the audience? ah,
there isn't one, so the applause must be canned, so when
William G Stewart says thank you to the audience, he's saying
thank you to eleven people and a canned applause machine,
Christ it's hot, stand behind your number (drawn by lots, all
fair and above board), someone tells us not to lean into microphone because they will be able to hear us perfectly, some
people will lean into microphone anyway because they can't
help it, everyone wishing they were somewhere else, several
wishing they were someone else, just as long as I'm not
knocked out in the first round, please god please god I know
I don't believe in you but for fuck's sake look after me now,
not the first round, I promise to get everything wrong in the
second round just as long as you give me an easy question in
the first round. Lights up. Hotter than ever. Theme music.

William G Stewart turns to camera. Reads autocue. The horror begins.

Except that, when it does begin, it's not actually that horrible. The ordeal quickly becomes a game, and games are there to be played. Adrenalin is your friend: it obliterates all distractions. I am at number 10 in the semi-circle. The previous winner is at number 4, and so answers his first question before me. He has an easy one to start. 'Which word can describe a company of actors playing roles, the throw of a fishing line or a defect in the eye?' Lucky bastard, I think. 'Cast,' he says without pause. You each get two questions in the first round: answer one correctly and you survive to the second. Soon it is my turn.

*'Wine. From which European country do the wines of
Bardolino, Frascati and Lambrusco originate?'*

Italy. Correct. Utter relief. Go to sleep until it's my turn again. The questions continue around the semi-circle, reach the end, start again from the beginning. Number 3 sits down! He has got both his questions wrong! Everyone else very happy about this. They may yet fail, but the main thing is that someone else has failed first. Number 3 now looking worried. It's bad enough to be knocked out in the first round, but it's far far worse to be the only person to be knocked out in the first round. He is sweating, and I don't blame him.

Previous winner at number 4 makes a mistake. 'Shakespeare. Spoken by Orsino, Duke of Illyria, "If music be the food of love, play on" is the first line of which play?' *Twelfth Night.* Easy. He says *As You Like It.* I try not to cry 'Yowsah!' and dance on the spot. Fatal lapse of concentration. At least, that's my excuse.

*'Which French king, known as the Sun King, was fond of
dancing and singing but saw no point in reading?'*

I am pretty certain this is Louis XIV. My friend Esther was
once on the TV version of Trivial Pursuit. She told me afterwards of the way your mind tells you one answer (correct) and
your mouth says another, completely different answer (wrong).
This now happens. Gripped by panic and self-doubt, I say
Louis XVI. What am I thinking of? Perhaps this is what happened to the previous winner at number 4 with his *Twelfth
Night* question. I have lost one life; I have two lives left.

Other people's questions are so *bloody* easy. 'A quincunx is a
symmetrical arrangement of how many objects?' What else
can it be but five? ' "Absence makes the heart . . ." do what?'
Oh, for Christ's sake. Other people's easy questions you resent;
other people's hard questions you ignore, unless they get them
right, in which case you look at them with new respect. As it
is, after round one only two contestants have been eliminated.
The remaining thirteen will play for the three places in today's
final.

In round two the format changes. Now, if you answer a
question correctly, you nominate the next person to be asked
one. Amazingly the first four all get their answers wrong,
including the previous winner. Ha ha, you self-satisfied git! A
few more shockingly easy questions ('What is the acronym for
Missile Defence Alarm System?' Er, would that be MIDAS by
any chance?) but many more stinkers, for this is the round that
must cast off the most players. Previous winner goes first,
then the man at number 2, and still I haven't been nominated.
The woman at number 7 finally notices me. The cow, the
ratbag, the unprincipled, wizened old trout.

*'A creature or plant described as being stagnicolous lives where
specifically?'*

Never heard of the word; time for a wild guess. 'Um, well, a
stagnant pond?' I proffer. 'Exactly,' says William G Stewart. I

nod slowly, as though I had known this all the time. Now I get
to do the nominating. I look around and string out the tension
a bit, although I had already decided to nominate the woman
at 15 several questions ago. She gets hers wrong. Next, the
man at 13. 'Its capital city is Kathmandu, the monetary unit is
the rupee, and the chief of state is King Birendra. Which
country is that?'[1] He doesn't know. I'm developing a taste for
this. I nominate the woman at 6, but for some reason she gets
hers right. A swirl of questions, nominations, right answers,
wrong answers. Two more are eliminated. There are nine of
us left, and I still have two lives. The woman at 6 remembers
me. I had nominated her before; now she wreaks bitter
revenge.

*'In which opera by Puccini does Minnie fall in love with an
outlaw in California during the Gold Rush era?'*

Mind goes blank. Eyes revolve in sockets. Look on video
recording like badly animated soft toy. 'It's called *The Girl of
the Golden West*,' says William G Stewart, clearly shocked that
I have never heard of it. (I have now.) More questions and
answers, more players knocked out. There are six players left.
Five of us have one life left, and the man at 9 still has two.
The woman at 15 nominates me.

*'How many nations signed the Charter of the United Nations
in San Francisco in June 1945?'*

They say a hunted animal always knows when it's going to
die. As soon as I hear William G Stewart say the words 'How
many . . .', I know I am fucked. 'Five?' I say. 'Fifty,' he says.

---

[1] Nepal.

'Uh!' I grunt, and sit down, angry and disappointed. In the end the men at 8 and 9 and the woman at 15 go through to the final, as I sit behind the camera and dream up ways of disposing of their dismembered corpses.

Had I been Trevor Montague, I would now have started planning for my next appearance, possibly by shaving my head and gluing on a false moustache. It was in fact two years before the phone rang. By this time I was working as TV critic and columnist for the *Daily Mail*, and in the course of normal professional life had bumped into 'Bill' Stewart several times. He knew I would sell both of my grandmothers to appear on the show again. So when his office rang up on a Monday morning and asked me whether I would go on a 'celebrity' edition of the show to be recorded that afternoon, it was all I could do not to break down and weep with gratitude.

There was only one small problem. Her name was Jo and I had a hot date with her for lunch. She worked in Brussels and had flown to London for the weekend. She was flying back that afternoon; this was my only opportunity to see her. Our relationship, such as it was, was at a crucial juncture. But *Fifteen-To-One* wanted me for their 'celebrity' edition. Vincent Hanna had dropped out at the last minute. 'But I'm not a celebrity,' I said, hoping they hadn't noticed. 'Doesn't matter,' said the woman from Regent Productions, 'we've got a couple of other TV critics, and they're not celebrities either.' Clearly some barrels had been scraped for this, and I was at the bottom of the very last barrel. But I am not a proud man, so I signed up. I never saw Jo again. Who knows what might have happened to us had Vincent Hanna not intervened?

To a recording of a normal edition of *Fifteen-To-One* you travel on the Tube. For a celebrity edition a black car the size of Basingstoke comes to pick you up. This, you feel, is how life should be lived, as long as someone else is paying for it. Had I not blown out a beautiful and intelligent woman who, until an hour before, had thought I was fab, I might have enjoyed the journey. But even she was momentarily forgotten when I arrived at the studio, which was knee-deep in faintly embarrassed celebrities (and Lionel Blair). William G Stewart had called in a few favours for this one. At lunch, which was mainly red wine, I sat with Lesley Joseph of *Birds of a Feather*, the comedian and presenter Rory McGrath, and Sue Carpenter, in those days an ITN newscaster. By the time my shyness had dissipated and I realised I was having a good time, it was too late: I was three sheets to the wind. Fortunately several others were at least four. When Rory McGrath told Sue Carpenter, 'You're the most beautiful Spurs fan I've ever met,' I knew this was going to be fun.

A glittering line-up was completed by Richard Whiteley of *Countdown*; Judi Spiers, then a presenter of *Pebble Mill*; Patrick Stoddart, then TV critic of the *Sunday Times*; Matthew Kelly of *Stars In Your Eyes*; Sally Jones, who had been a sportscaster on TV-am; the legendary Jim Bowen from *Bullseye*; Anna Raeburn (agony aunt, clearly suffering herself); Gyles Brandreth (minus sweater); Austin Mitchell MP (terrified his constituents might be watching); and John Inman. The international fellowship of TV fame meant that they had all met each other before, were thrilled to see each other again and kissed each other several times on the cheek. (Scene: Judi Spiers's house. The doorbell rings. Judi opens the door. It's the plumber. 'Darling!' she cries, opening her arms, 'haven't seen you for simply ages! Mwah! Mwah! Mwah!') In fact much of this bonhomie masked naked terror. Nothing the celebs had previously done had prepared them for this ordeal. 'But I don't know anything,' said at least three of them. Most had agreed in haste and were repenting over lunch. The drunk ones soon anaesthetised their worries; the sober ones grew ever more jittery. Matthew Kelly, in particular, appeared to be bricking himself. 'I quite enjoyed it the last time I was on,' I said, breezily. He looked at me as though I was mad. 'Do you mean to say that you are doing this again voluntarily?' he said, with a shudder.

Sadly, details of the actual quiz cannot be reproduced here, as all videotapes have since been systematically destroyed. As I remember it, I was knocked out 10th, having failed to identify three suburbs of Greater Humberside. Lesley Joseph and Judi Spiers somehow made it to the final, along with Patrick Stoddart, who hadn't been nominated to answer a single question in round two. (He had stepped back a pace out of everyone's eyeline, so they all forgot about him and nominated each other.) Stoddart won the final with relative ease.

Not surprisingly, this was the last 'celebrity' edition of *Fifteen-To-One*. If they needed me and Stoddart to make up the numbers, they must have been struggling. But it remains the highlight of my quizzing career so far. To stand in the same semicircle as such august personages and see them sit down with relief when they couldn't remember the capital of Botswana was a true privilege. I occasionally bump into Rory McGrath at parties and we grin knowingly at each other. We were on the 'celebrity' edition of *Fifteen-To-One* together. Only survivors of major air crashes can have a firmer bond.

And still the lure of the perfect quiz question drives us on. Only last night, when I should have been finishing this book, or sorting out my tax, or doing anything other than sitting in the pub with Terence, I sat in the pub with Terence and discussed the quiz we are compiling for next Tuesday. There was no need to: most of the questions are already written (or stolen), but I had come across a fact of such magnificence I had to share it with him. In an opinion poll conducted by the

Church of England in 1998 to establish who was the best-known Christian in the world, God came first. Who came second? Terence, in a flash of possibly divine inspiration, got it immediately.[2] We sat and basked in its warm glow. Bertrand Russell once said, 'What men really want is not knowledge but certainty.' What did he know? Men will happily forego certainty for the knowledge that of all tin cans sold in the British Isles, more than one in five contains baked beans. At least, that's my conviction. See you on Tuesday.

Answers to Quiz 10

Of Glasgow, Swansea and Plymouth the farthest west is Glasgow. The Poet Laureate from 1843 to 1850, who wrote no poems in those years, was William Wordsworth. The London Underground station with the same name as a station on the Paris Metro is Temple. The Queen was born on 21 April which makes her a Taurus. And the tie-breaker: the first recorded (i.e. written) use of the word 'pig' to describe a policeman was as far back as 1812.

---

[2] Sir Cliff Richard. Mother Teresa came third, the Pope ninth.

*Ted Rogers: 'This is a composer, German by birth, English by
   adoption, best known for an oratorio published in 1741.'
   Short pause. 'It was called . . .* Messiah.' *Longer pause.
   'You're bound to know . . . his handle.'
Both teams press buzzers.
Ted: 'Who is it?'
Female contestant (shutting eyes): 'Oh God, I used to have it at
   school . . . Handel's* Water Music . . .'
*Ted: 'So who's the composer?'
Female contestant: 'Chopin.'
Uproar from audience.
Ted (turning to other team): 'So I can offer it to you.'
Male contestant: 'Beethoven?'*

                                        (3-2-1, Yorkshire TV, 1977)

Acknowledgements

Thanks to many friends and quizmates who helped, gave advice and bought drinks, in particular Terence Russoff, Chris Pollikett and George Clark, whose good names I have traduced for my own ends; to Russell Taylor and Tara Spring, for all the best questions in the quiz sections; to Michael Barfield, for many good ideas and particular help on the 'Childhood' chapter; also to Cliff Allen, Stephen Arkell, Charlie Blythe, Mark Brisenden, Will Buckley, Matthew Burrows, Richard Corden, Ian Hislop, Corinna Honan, Mark Jacobs, David Jaques, Esther Kaposi, Julia Kreitman, Barry Kyle, Andy Leonard, David McCandless, Howard McMinn, Gerry Masters, Lucy Maycock, Chris Millington, Simon O'Hagan, John Osmond, Ged Parsons, Lucy Reese, Judy Reith, Andy Robson, Simon Rose, Kate Saunders, Phil South, Richard Spence, Boyd Steemson, William G Stewart and Regent Productions, Patrick Stoddart, Mitchell Symons, David

Taylor, David Thomas, Tanja van der Putten, Patrick Walsh, Robin Welch and Ceili Williams; to my mother Jean Berkmann-Barwis, the only person I knew who was bound to have kept videotapes of me on *Fifteen-To-One* (even if she had inadvertently taped *The Camomile Lawn* over one of them); to Burns & Porter for permission to reprint their questions; to Richard Beswick, Antonia Hodgson and everyone at Little, Brown for their trust and support; and to Paula Bingham for the title and much more besides.

A Selective Index

Orthos, the two-headed dog of Geryon, 11
Osbourne, Ozzy, ate Orthos for dinner, 50

Parr, Catherine, sixth wife, 3
Paxman, Jeremy, 'patience of Job,' say doctors, 38, 67
Perks, Sid, has purchased quiz book, 120, 121
Pipkin, Inigo, not an architect, 90
Plato, constantly mistaken for cartoon dog, 12
Pluto, very rarely mistaken for Greek philosopher, 12
Powell, Robert, unable to bestow Christly favours, 181
Presley, Elvis, actually dead, 66
Purves, Peter, loves dogs, 97

Queen, no one was convinced by 'Fat Bottomed Girls', 27

Ra, Egyptian sun-god, 79
Ramsay, Sir Alf, good advice, 191
Redford, Robert, early quiz obsessive, 63
Reeves, Keanu, loathed by all heterosexual males, 12
Richard, Sir Cliff, only tennis player mentioned by name in text, 12
Rodd, Michael, presented *Screen Test*, 96
Roger, Ted, purple, 70; with laughter, 206
Russell, Bertrand, wrong again, 205
Russon, Chris, always runner-up to Anthony Martin, 73

St Benedict, dial 999, 87
St Bernardine of Siena, poor poor woman, 87
St Bibiana, her round, 87
St Francis of Assisi, rarely cheated in pub quizzes, 124
St George, *sans* dragon, 87
St Maurice, 24-hour service, 87
St Nicholas, spreads himself thin, 87
Scott, Sir Walter, name lives on only in quiz questions, 10
Sex Pistols, The, a long long time ago, 24
Shakespeare, William, first name not 'Arthur', as suggested by *Family
    Fortunes* contestant, 83–5
Sharkey, Feargal, on George's team, 31; not on George's team, 33
Simon Peter, no one likes a smartarse, 13, 14
Socrates, mispronounced by an entire generation, 12
Soros, George, secret quizzing past, 24
Sphinx, The, peckish, 11